The Real Roadrunner

ANIMAL NATURAL HISTORY SERIES

Victor H. Hutchison, General Editor

The
Real
Roadrunner

MARTHA ANNE MAXON

UNIVERSITY OF OKLAHOMA PRESS : NORMAN

Library of Congress Cataloging-in-Publication Data

Maxon, Martha Anne, 1941–
    The real roadrunner / Martha Anne Maxon.
      p.   cm. — (Animal natural history series)
    Includes bibliographical references (p.).
    ISBN 0-8061-3676-6 (alk. paper)
    1. Roadrunner. I. Title. II. Series.

QL696.C83M39 2005
598.7'4—dc 22

                                        2005041716

The Real Roadrunner is Volume 9 in the Animal Natural History Series.

The paper in this book meets the guidelines for permanance and durability of the Committee on Production Guidelines for Book Longevity of the Council on Library Resources, Inc. ∞

1 2 3 4 5 6 7 8 9 10

To the memory of my father, Byron Martin White, DVM,
who loved wild things and taught me to love them,
and
to the memory of Dr. George Miksch Sutton,
who loved the roadrunner and taught me to love it.

Contents

Illustrations

Plates

the roadrunner, which occupies its time for three-fourths of the year and illustrates the adaptable nature of this species. Understanding the natural history of the roadrunner sets the stage for exploring the reasons for its ability to expand its range five hundred miles eastward from its desert home into the heartland of the United States during the last century. Besides the bird's adaptability, human changes to the landscape may have helped in its eastward trek. Barriers to its further eastward and northern expansion may exist, however, and we will examine them to round out our understanding of the roadrunner's natural history.

Because this bird has been so intimately connected with various cultures for many centuries and is popular in modern culture, I have included a final chapter on the colorful folklore and tales about the roadrunner. The roadrunner is one of the icons of the Southwest and one of the most loved birds of our country.

In this book, for ease of reading, I use the term 'roadrunner' rather than its official common name, "greater roadrunner." For those who are interested, the scientific names of plants and animals mentioned in the text are placed in the index, under the common name of each species.

The sources I have used appear in the bibliography. Approximately two-thirds of these are cited in the text. The remainder provided background information, and I have included them in the interest of completeness.

Acknowledgments

Along the way, I have been helped by many wonderful people too numerous to name. But I will attempt to acknowledge as many as I can.

Lawrence E. Maxon, my beloved husband, who never ceased to be my support and anchor throughout the writing of this book

Dr. Byron Martin White and Ione Bullard White, my late father and mother, who helped me watch roadrunners and find nests and gave me a childhood full of the wonders of nature

Byron White, my brother, who faithfully read most of this manuscript and provided comments and constant encouragement

Dr. George Miksch Sutton (deceased), University of Oklahoma, who first taught me about the wonders of roadrunner-watching and shared many of his insights and questions about the bird, as well as his experiences in raising pet roadrunners as a young boy

Dr. Frederick R. Gehlbach, Baylor University, who gave me an ecological viewpoint

Dr. Charles C. Carpenter, University of Oklahoma, who taught me the principles of animal behavior, field observation, and time-motion analysis of behavior

Dr. Victor Hutchison, general editor of the University of Oklahoma Press's Animal Natural History Series, who provided editorial guidance

Dr. Gary Schnell, University of Oklahoma, who provided several Oklahoma references

Dr. Matthew C. Perry, Patuxent Wildlife Research Center, who spent time in a musty government storage room digging out the old U.S. Biological Survey food habits cards for the roadrunner and supplied them to me

Dr. Wade C. Sherbrooke, American Museum of Natural History, Southwestern Research Station, Portal, Arizona, who discussed his horned lizard and roadrunner research with me

Polly Schaafsma, anthropologist and artist of Santa Fe, New Mexico, who took time to discuss American Indian petroglyphs and folklore with me

Dr. Elizabeth Brandt, Arizona State University, who discussed American Indian folklore with me and directed me to major literature sources

Barbie Coselman, who thoughtfully read this manuscript from the point of view of a layperson and a top-notch secretary and gave me invaluable suggestions on content and grammar

Terry van de Walle, who enthusiastically conducted the records search for past and current roadrunner distribution

Dr. Janice M. Hughes, who shared her insights on cuckoo phylogeny and her observations and enthusiasm for the roadrunner

James D. Lowe, Cornell Laboratory of Ornithology, Cornell University, who provided the nest record card data from the lab's Bird Population Studies database

Kathy Klimkiewicz, Bird Banding Laboratory, Patuxent Wildlife Research Center, Laurel, Maryland, who provided bird-banding data

Jan Bird, Kimberly Gilbert, Willie Graham, Jewel Schultheis, and Pat and Dick Weekly, all dear friends whose friendship and prayers saw me through to the end

Jacque Staston, graphic artist, who digitally edited plates 1–4, 10, 11, 16, and 21 in this book and shares my enthusiasm for roadrunners

Ione Prange and Janice Holmes, librarians who tracked down many of the reference articles used for this book

Staff of the University of Oklahoma Press who guided this manuscript to completion, including Kimberly Wiar, Jean Hurtado, Karen C. Wieder, and Marian Stewart

Rosemary Wetherold, another roadrunner fan, who did a magnificent job as copy editor of the book

The many volunteers who have contributed to our knowledge of roadrunner nesting habits by participating in the North American Nest Record Card Program, and especially to Mr. and Mrs. Orphus C. Bone, who covered five counties in the South Texas brushlands between 1967 and 1974 and provided almost a third of the roadrunner records

The following providers of financial support for my roadrunner field research over the years: a National Park Service Research Grant, an NSF Grant-in-Aid at the University of Oklahoma Biological Station, and the National Geographic Society

Illustration Credits

Curtis Schaafsma (provided by Polly Schaafsma): figure 18.

Dr. Wade Sherbrooke: plates 5, 6, and 9.

All other photographs are my own.

All drawings are by Mark Hughes, Hudson, Quebec, Canada, with the exception of figures 5, 15, and 16, which are my own.

The Real Roadrunner

1

Roadrunner Basics

Writing this book has brought back wonderful memories of time I spent with the roadrunner in Texas and New Mexico. Looking back, I realize how privileged I have been to observe the life of this amazing bird in its natural habitat. I also raised several of these birds in captivity as part of my study of their courtship behavior for my doctoral dissertation. Altogether, I spent six breeding seasons with these birds, involving thousands of hours of observation and many still photographs and movie films of behavior and tape recordings of calls. I feel privileged to share what I and others have learned about this intriguing bird with the readers of this book.

My romance with the roadrunner began when I was a child growing up in the brush country of South Texas. I was fortunate to have a father who loved the animals and land of this area of Texas. Our family's outings were spent learning about the wild things around us. One of the creatures that fascinated me the most was the roadrunner, whose charisma entrances those fortunate enough to encounter it. It is hard to pin down exactly what facets of this complex bird grab one's attention, but no one who has spent time with this bird remains dispassionate about it, whether scientist or layperson. My hope is that this book will acquaint the reader with the life of the roadrunner and stimulate interest in helping uncover its many secrets that still elude us.

Although the roadrunner is an icon of the Southwest and beloved by people throughout the world, it has been one of the most misunderstood of birds. This misunderstanding has come about not only because ideas about the roadrunner are colored by centuries of folklore and the twentieth-century animated character but also because little knowledge existed about the real bird until relatively recently. Roadrunner research of the last fifty years has revealed a real creature every bit as fascinating as the legend and cartoon, if not more so. As the first step on our journey to know the real roadrunner, we begin with its discovery by Euro-American people.

An anonymous Franciscan priest wrote the first known description of the roadrunner in 1790. His account appeared in a Spanish manuscript containing memories of California's natural history: "The *Churca* is a kind of pheasant which has a long bill, dark plumage, a handsome tail and *four feet*. It has these latter facing outward in such fashion that when it runs it leaves the track of two feet going forward and two going backward" (quoted in Coues 1900, 70; note that the "four feet" could be a mistranslation of the Spanish). Although an astute observer of the roadrunner's anatomy, this priest made the same mistake that many casual observers of this bird do: grouping it with the pheasant.

The next report comes from famous explorer Lieutenant Zebulon Montgomery Pike, who caught a roadrunner in 1806 in Chaffee County, Colorado (A. M. Bailey and Niedrach 1965). However, it wasn't until 1829 that French naturalist and surgeon René-Primevère Lesson provided the first scientific description of the bird from a San Diego County, California, specimen. He gave it the scientific name *Saurothera californiana,* correctly identifying it as a member of the cuckoo family. Its placement in the genus *Saurothera* allied the roadrunner with several distantly related New World cuckoos, the lizard-cuckoos.

In 1831 the roadrunner was placed in the new genus *Geococcyx,* along with a newly discovered species, the lesser roadrunner, *Geococcyx velox.* Between then and 1858 the roadrunner was known by various scientific names, including *Geococcyx variegata, G. mexicanus, G. viaticus, G. marginatus,* and *G. californicus* (Ridgway 1916).

Geococcyx californianus, the current scientific name for the roadrunner, was established in 1858 by Spencer Fullerton Baird, assistant secretary of the Smithsonian Institution (and later its director). The genus name means "earth *[geo]* cuckoo *[coccyx]*." The type specimen came from California; hence the species name *californianus*. The official common name for the species is "greater roadrunner," to distinguish it from the lesser roadrunner. In this book, the term "roadrunner" is used to refer to the greater roadrunner. When the lesser roadrunner is mentioned, its full common name is used.

Roadrunner Roots

As a background for the natural history of the roadrunner, we will look at it in the context of its cuckoo family. First impressions can deceive observers into thinking that the roadrunner is a fowl, that is, a cousin to the quail, the pheasant, and the chicken. But its ground-dwelling habit and drab appearance are misleading, for the roadrunner is a genuine member of the cuckoo clan. However, this earthbound bird is a nonconformist, standing in stark contrast to its aerial, tree-dwelling cuckoo relatives.

Figure. 1. Yellow-billed cuckoo.

To most, the word "cuckoo" brings to mind either a cuckoo clock or a crazy idea or person. In fact, the cuckoo-clock bird is patterned after the European cuckoo. The cuckoo is named for the *cuc-coo*ing courtship call of the male European cuckoo. Because this bird gives his cry repeatedly, even late into the night, "cuckoo" came to describe something or someone dull, foolish, or crazy (Amon 1978).

The order Cuculiformes, to which both the roadrunner and the European cuckoo belong, is a varied assortment of species. Besides the worldwide-occurring cuckoos, this group includes the coucals of Africa and Asia, the couas of Madagascar, and the anis and ground-cuckoos of the Americas. This is the only order of birds with living species of tree dwellers that are strong fliers and ground dwellers that are weak fliers. The other ground-dwelling birds, such as the ostrich and the emu, do not have living tree-dwelling relatives. The ground-dwelling quail, pheasant, and grouse are good fliers, unlike the ground-dwelling cuckoos.

Close comparison of roadrunner features with those of other cuckoos, such as the yellow-billed cuckoo, reveals many similarities. Can you see resemblances between the roadrunner in plates 1–4 and the yellow-billed cuckoo in figure 1? Cuckoo species, whether tree-dwelling or ground-dwelling, share a set of physical characteristics, including the following:

Long, stout, downward-curving bill
Long, slender tail with white spots on tips of tail feathers

Figure 2. Zygodactyl
foot of roadrunner.

Figure 3. Rufous-vented ground-cuckoo.

Zygodactyl foot, which has two toes pointing forward and two backward (fig. 2)

Naked, two-lobed oil gland at the tip of the tail bone

Bare patch of skin, usually colored, in the area behind the eye, having the effect of emphasizing the eye

Rather drab plumage, often streaked

Eyelashes

Look-alike sexes

Hatchlings naked or with sparse, hairlike strands on the body

Thirty-six genera, containing 139 cuckoo species, are found throughout the warm and temperate areas of the world. A special aspect of cuckoo biology that has received attention from research biologists is brood parasitism, which occurs when the cuckoo species lays its eggs in the nest of another bird species. The host bird incubates the eggs and cares for the cuckoo young, usually at the expense of its own eggs or offspring. Often the color and pattern of the cuckoo egg match those of the host bird's eggs. About 40 percent of cuckoo species practice brood parasitism.

Roadrunners are part of the Neomorphinae, the ground-cuckoos/roadrunner subfamily of cuckoos. Cuckoo species in this subfamily occur only in the Americas. These species share features related to their ground-dwelling habit—long, strong legs and short wings. The long tail of the tree-dwelling cuckoos provides balance for perching and flying, and that of the ground-cuckoos provides stability as they walk or run. The species considered most closely related to the roadrunner are in the genus *Neomorphus*. Figure 3 shows one of these species, the rufous-vented ground-cuckoo of Central and South America. Table 1 provides general information about the Neomorphinae.

The earliest known ground-dwelling cuckoo fossil is that of *Cursoricoccyx geraldinae* from a Colorado site. It is placed in the Neomorphinae group and may be closely related to today's roadrunner species (Martin and Mengel 1984).

Among the Neomorphinae, the roadrunner is the only species whose natural history is well known. The secretive habits, remote locations, and densely vegetated tropical or subtropical habitats of most of the ground-cuckoos make them hard to observe. Also, little information exists on the lesser roadrunner, despite its more accessible range and habitat. Information on a few ground-cuckoos appears in several places in this book for comparison with the roadrunner's natural history.

Another roadrunner, Conkling's roadrunner, once roamed the Southwest during the late Pleistocene. Bone measurements indicate that this bird could have been 10 to 20 percent larger than the modern roadrunner. Paleontologists now consider it to be a subspecies *(Geococcyx californianus conklingi)* of the fossil, modern-sized form, *Geococcyx californianus californianus,* which occurred at that time as well (Harris and Crews 1983; Carpenter and Mead 2003).

It is thought that there was some geographic separation of the two subspecies. To date, the majority of *G. c. californianus* fossils have come from Southern California, especially along the western coast, whereas the fossils of Conkling's roadrunner have come from

TABLE 1
General range and habitat of the roadrunner and its ground-cuckoo relatives

Scientific name Common name Length	General range	General habitat
Tapera naevia Striped cuckoo 11–12"	Mexico to Argentina	Dense thickets, brushy fields
Morococcyx erythropygus Lesser groud-cuckoo 10"	Mexico, Guatemala, El Salvador, Honduras, Nicaragua, Costa Rica	Arid woodlands, thickets, shrubby fields
Dromococcyx phasianellus Pheasant cuckoo 15–16"	Brazil, Peru, Colombia, Venezuela, Paraguay	Dense forest undergrowth, thickets, humid forest edges
Dromococcyx pavoninus Pavonine cuckoo 10"	Brazil, Peru, Bolivia, Venezuela, Paraguay	Tropical rain forests
Geococcyx californianus Greater roadrunner 22–24"	United States, Mexico	Desert scrub, shrubby fields, open woods, riparian woods
Geococcyx velox Lesser roadrunner 20–22"	Mexico, Guatemala, El Salvador, Honduras, Nicaragua	Arid scrub, thickets, open woods
Neomorphus geoffroyi Rufous-vented ground-cuckoo 19–20"	Nicaragua, Costa Rica, Panama, Colombia, Ecuador, Peru, Bolivia, Brazil	Tropical rain forest
Neomorphus squamiger Scaled ground-cuckoo 19–20"	Brazil	Tropical rain forest
Neomorphus radiolosus Banded ground-cuckoo 19–20"	Colombia, Ecuador	Lowland tropical rain forest, montane tropical rain forest
Neomorphus rufipennis Rufous-winged ground-cuckoo 19–20"	Venezuela, Brazil, Guyana, Colombia	Tropical rain forest
Neomorphus pucheranii Red-billed ground-cuckoo 18"	Brazil, Peru	Tropical rain forest

Sources: Haffner 1977; Phelps and de Schauensee 1978; Willis 1982; American Ornithologists' Union 1983; Dunning 1987; S. N. G. Howell and Webb 1995.

southern New Mexico (Howard 1931), West Texas (Gehlbach and Holman 1974), and north-eastern Mexico (Steadman et al. 1994). Recently, the westernmost specimen of Conkling's roadrunner was found in Kartchner Caverns State Park in southeastern Arizona (Carpenter and Mead 2003). This roadrunner became extinct in the early Holocene (about six thousand years ago) when the climate was becoming warmer and drier.

No recognized subspecies of the roadrunner exist today. Several ornithologists have examined the possibility of a modern, slightly smaller subspecies, with its distribution in the eastern part of the species' range (Oberholser 1974; J. M. Hughes 1996a). Janice Hughes found that East Texas males were significantly smaller than California males in overall length and in wing, tarsus, tail, and bill lengths. Although such a subspecies is not recognized to date, perhaps a broadly clinal variation exists, with eastern birds being slightly smaller and darker and having larger white tips on the outer tail feathers than western birds (Pyle 1997).

Geared for the Ground

Weighing slightly less than a pound, the roadrunner is nearly two feet in length, half of which is tail, and it stands nine to ten inches tall (plate 1). Adult weights range from ten to twenty-one ounces (J. M. Hughes 1996a). At a distance, the bird appears to have brownish, dull, streaked plumage, but at close range, its true colors show. The dark, white-fringed feathers are glossy and iridescent, with colors of olive, bronze, steel blue-black, brown or black, depending on the lighting. The upper breast feathers are a streaked mixture of buff, brown, black, and white, and the lower breast and abdomen feathers are pale gray.

A large, white spot brightens the tips of all but the two center tail feathers (plates 4 and 8). There is also a white spot near the middle of each wing feather, which show when the wings are spread. These spots are visible on the wings of the sunning bird in plate 8.

As expected for a ground-dwelling bird, a greater amount of the roadrunner's body is devoted to moving on its feet than to using its wings. Almost a quarter of its body mass is in its leg muscles, and only about 14 percent in its wing muscles. The opposite is true for the average flying bird, which has about a quarter of its body mass devoted to flying muscles and 9 percent to leg muscles (Calder 1984).

Comparing the body of the roadrunner with that of several of its tree-dwelling cuckoo relatives, ornithologist Andrew Berger (1952, 1954) found that the roadrunner's pelvic bones were larger, its thigh muscles were better developed, and its breast muscles were less developed. He concluded that the major factors contributing to roadrunner speed are its very long legs and its alternate leg action. In addition, he found that several pelvic muscles originate farther forward and to the side in the roadrunner than in tree-dwelling cuckoos, improving the roadrunner's balance during alternate leg movements. Figure 4 shows the leg and wing proportions of the roadrunner.

The feet are about two and one-half inches long, with two toes pointing forward and two pointing backward, a pattern called zygodactyl (fig. 2). Unlike some birds that can move their outer toe either forward or backward as needed, the cuckoo's outer rear toe is

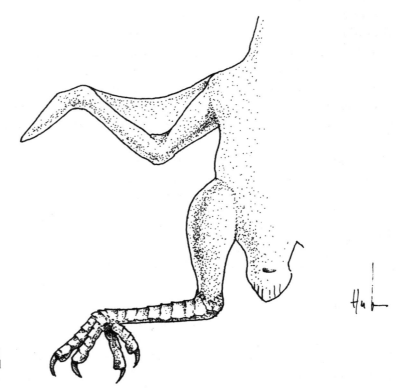

Figure 4. Wing and leg
of roadrunner. Adapted
from Shufeldt 1886b.

permanently in the rear position. In tree-dwelling cuckoos, this foot pattern is considered an
adaptation for perching. However, the muscle that controls the toe extension in the roadrunner is longer than that of tree-dwelling cuckoos, allowing the toes to spread out on a flat
surface (Berger 1952). This trait doesn't stop the roadrunner from using its feet for perching,
and it spends considerable time in trees while foraging and nesting.

The long cuckoo tail, useful for balancing on perches and flying, is also an asset to the
roadrunner's running movements. During nonstop straight running, the roadrunner holds
its head and tail parallel to the ground, but it fans and tips its tail to maneuver during
zigzag running and it lifts the tail to help brake. Other uses for the tail are as a foil when
fighting, a brace and thrusting force when jumping, and a showy visual signal during courtship display.

Several biologists, intrigued by this bird's swiftness, measured its speed with a car and
reported rates of fifteen to twenty miles per hour (Hunt 1920; Sheldon 1922; Cottam, Williams,
and Sooter 1942). Researchers Kavanau and Ramos (1970) reported that roadrunners on an
activity wheel could maintain running speeds of greater than eighteen miles per hour. These
are extremely fast speeds for a bird lighter than a pound with feet that are only two and one-
half inches long. The much larger ostrich has been clocked at a running speed of thirty-one

miles per hour and up to forty-four miles per hour for short bursts. I marvel at the roadrunner's ability to sustain its pace on the hot desert ground.

The roadrunner can fly, but its flight is limited by its long, heavy legs and short, weak wings. It flies only short distances, usually starting from a fast run. Its typical flight is a wing-and-tail glide to the ground from a high perch, such as a cliff, a treetop, or a building. The longest flight I have witnessed was a glide from a high West Texas cliff across the Rio Grande onto the river-bank in Mexico, a ground distance of about a quarter mile. Roadrunners also glide short distances on the ground, taking off from a fast running start with wings furiously flapping.

Unlike most other cuckoos, the roadrunner sports a large, moveable crest. This shaggy topknot is usually flattened (plate 1) but is raised when the bird is alerted, agitated, or courting (plate 2). The roadrunner's most colorful feature is the inch-long patch of bare skin located around and behind the eye, extending to the back of the head (plates 2 and 3). This area is an indigo blue around the eye, and behind the eye it is white to bluish white with a blue edging. Following around the head, the color abruptly changes to a bright chrome orange. Unless the bird is agitated or courting, the orange area is usually not exposed, for it is covered by surrounding, small feathers (not by the crest, as has sometimes been described by other authors).

A keen observer may detect a roadrunner's level of agitation by paying attention to the amount of color patch that the bird exposes and the degree to which the crest is erected. The many possible crest positions can combine with differing amounts of color patch exposure to produce a variety of patterns. Some of these variations are shown in figure 5 and plates 2 and 3. These patterns could be signals in roadrunner language, but if so, their meanings are unknown to us. The color patch is most often exposed during the male's courtship behavior, described in chapter 4.

Another prominent head feature is the long, stout bill with a hooked tip, colored from dark charcoal to brown. It is a powerful one-and-a-half-inch weapon for capturing and killing prey (plate 6). The mouth of the adult is solid black, in contrast to the bright reddish pink mouth of the nestling.

Roadrunner sexes are nearly impossible to tell apart in the field by appearance alone. Females average about an ounce lighter and are slightly under an inch shorter than males, but these differences are not discernible in the field. Folse and Arnold (1976) reported a subtle color difference in the bare skin around and behind the eye of roadrunners in South Texas. The females had a light blue to medium blue bare area behind the eye, whereas in the males the area was white or bluish white. This color difference was also difficult to discern, except at very close range and after having gained experience by observing a number of roadrunner pairs. Folse and Arnold cautioned that the color difference was based on only one popula-tion of roadrunners. They reported one successful nest where both parents had a white color behind the eye. Further study is needed on the amount of color variation overlap between the sexes and on the geographic variation of this feature.

For both captive and wild birds, I was able to confirm the sex of birds only by their behavior during copulation in the breeding season. Individuals were identified by features such as missing tail feathers.

Figure 5. Variations of crest erection and color patch display: *a*, crest normal, color obscured; *b*, crest sleeked, exposed color; *c*, crest slightly erect, color exposed; *d*, crest moderately erect, color partially obscured; *e*, crest fully erect, color fully exposed; *f*, anterior view of e; *g*, posterior view of *e*.

At a distance, the roadrunner looks like the lesser roadrunner, but the former is two to four inches longer and has belly feathers that are grayish white rather than buff-colored, as in the lesser roadrunner. The lesser roadrunner's foreneck and central chest area are not streaked, as they are in the roadrunner. If visible, the bare area behind the eye can help distinguish between the species, for it is blue, grading to crimson, in the lesser roadrunner.

Geographic Range

The roadrunner is a nonmigratory species that normally moves only locally within a small area throughout its life. Despite this limitation, the species extended its range from its southwestern home into the Midwest and several southeastern states during the last century. Today it occurs in twelve states in the United States and in Mexico. The northern limits of its range extend through Northern California, southern Nevada, southeastern Utah, southeastern

Colorado, central Kansas, and south-central Missouri. (Records from the four-corners area where Arizona, New Mexico, Colorado, and Utah join are old and scant, and this region is not considered a part of the current range.) Eastern limits extend into central Missouri, eastern Arkansas, and northeastern, central, and southwestern Louisiana.

The bird's range also extends through much of northern and central Mexico, stretching from the Gulf of Mexico to the Gulf of California and across Baja California to the Pacific Ocean. The lesser roadrunner occurs in the northwestern part of the Yucatán Peninsula and the western areas of the countries of Mexico, Belize, Guatemala, El Salvador, Honduras, and Nicaragua. The roadrunner's range overlaps slightly with that of the lesser roadrunner in a small slice of southwestern Mexico in the states of Sonora, Sinaloa, Jalisco, and Michoacán (S. N. G. Howell and Webb 1995).

The roadrunner occurs at elevations ranging from 250 feet below sea level in Death Valley, California, to more than 11,000 feet high in the Rocky Mountains of Colorado. In most locations, however, it occurs below 7,000 feet.

Habitat

Unlike most birds living in northern temperate climates, roadrunners do not migrate south in the winter but are permanent residents and breeders wherever they occur. In their year-round homes, they face the challenges of adapting to seasonal temperature changes and finding adequate food and shelter in the winter months. Thus they are limited to geographic areas that are favorable to both successful nesting and winter survival.

That they have been able to expand their range and survive year-round in scorching deserts and areas with harsh winters says much about the adaptability of this bird. This habitat adaptability also suggests that the roadrunner cannot be characterized as an exclusively desert-dwelling bird, as it is popularly depicted.

Major roadrunner habitat types include desert scrub, chaparral, savanna, open brushlands, open woodlands, and wooded stream corridors. They live in myriad plant communities, including paloverde desert scrub, blackbrush scrub, cholla grassland, chaparral, mesquite scrub, mesquite savanna, juniper savanna, piñon-juniper woodland, juniper-oak woodland, pine-oak woodland, oak-hickory woodland, cedar glades, streamside woods, and salt cedar thickets. Roadrunners even adapt to living alongside humans in less densely populated urban and suburban areas, such as yards, parks, agricultural lands, and vacant lots. They rarely occur in dense, unvegetated urban areas, dense brushlands, or woodlands with thick undergrowth.

Considering the general vegetation structure of roadrunner habitats, all are similar—a mix of open area with aboveground, sturdy vegetation. The ground cover may range from bare ground to sparse, short bunchgrass or short lawn grass, while the taller vegetation may be cacti, small bushes, or trees.

The open areas are essential for maneuvers to flush and catch fast-moving insects and other prey. Open areas are also important during nesting, for they provide nearby foraging places where the parents can monitor the eggs and the young. Tall vegetation or artificial structures provide a safe place for nesting and roosting.

Populations

Roadrunners occur alone during the late fall and winter and in breeding pairs or small family groups during the breeding season. The roadrunner is not common anywhere the species occurs, but it is relatively more common in southwestern desert and brush habitats than in other parts of its range.

The North American Breeding Bird Survey indicates that the U.S. roadrunner population as a whole has been stable or only slightly declining since the survey started in the 1960s, although local population fluctuations are common (Sauer, Hines, and Fallow 2003). Populations along the northern limits of the species' range exhibit more fluctuations than elsewhere; fluctuations are associated with the severity of winter weather and the small numbers of individuals.

The roadrunner is protected by the U.S. Migratory Bird Treaty Act of 1918, which gives legal protection to nearly all U.S. birds, but there are probably a few places where roadrunners are still killed for sport or out of the belief that they are a threat to quail and to domestic chickens (Stimson 1975; Meinzer 1993).

The roadrunner is not federally or state-listed as threatened or endangered anywhere in its range. The Missouri Natural Heritage Database lists it as a species of conservation concern, with a rating of "sensitive 3" (rare and uncommon in the state, with between twenty-one and one hundred occurrences) (Missouri Department of Conservation 2003). The other northeastern and eastern states on the edge of the roadrunner's range do not list the bird as a sensitive species (Arkansas National Heritage Commission 2002; Louisiana Department of Wildlife and Fisheries, n.d.; Kansas Bird Records Committee 2002). Two ground-cuckoo relatives—the banded ground-cuckoo of Colombia and Ecuador and the scaled ground-cuckoo of Brazil—appear on the 2000 International Union for Conservation of Nature and Natural Resources Red List of Threatened Species (Hilton-Taylor 2000).

One might ask why the roadrunner is surviving when many other bird species are in peril. Unlike specialist birds, the roadrunner is not tied to a specific habitat or food, giving it flexibility to adapt to changes that humans make to the environment. The cause of extinction for many animals is destruction of their habitat or food supply, but the roadrunner is omnivorous and can survive in many habitats, including urban areas. I think that other reasons for its success are its parental skills and its ability to nest as many as three times in a breeding season.

Roadrunners are known to live for at least seven years in the wild. This longevity record is for a roadrunner that was banded as a nestling in central Oklahoma and found dead seven years and three months later only a few miles away from its hatching area (Patuxent Wildlife Research Center Bird Banding Laboratory, n.d.). A captive roadrunner lived to be nine years old in the Riverbanks Zoological Park in Columbia, South Carolina (Smith 1980). The U.S. longevity record for a cuckoo relative, the yellow-billed cuckoo, is five years in the wild.

The discussion of the natural history of the roadrunner presented in the rest of this book includes these and many other facets of this creature that have contributed to its success. First, we will look at how the roadrunner meets the basic survival needs of finding food (chapter 2) and protection from the elements and predators (chapter 3). Chapters 4–7 describe the events during courtship and nesting that contribute to the reproductive success of this species. In chapter 8 we look at how the adaptable nature of this species has enabled it to expand eastward. Chapter 9 gives a glimpse of the rich folklore associated with this bird and the reasons it has been popular for centuries in the past as well as in modern culture.

or eastern parts of the roadrunner's range. An important contribution to the natural history of the roadrunner would be observations on nestling diets in Kansas, Missouri, Arkansas, Louisiana, Colorado, Utah, and Northern California.

Quantities of Food

I am amazed at how much a roadrunner can cram into its stomach. For instance, Harold Bryant (1916) reported that a male roadrunner from Southern California had the following items in his stomach:

1 horned lizard
4 small lizards
12 small grasshoppers
4 large grasshoppers
50 tenebrionid beetles
1 weevil
10 carabid beetles
1 beetle larvae
2 moths

The quantity of venomous animals that one roadrunner can eat at a sitting is remarkable. One stomach contained 250 wasps, and another had 7 scorpions (Patuxent Wildlife Research Center, n.d.). No evidence has been found that roadrunners suffer ill effects from eating venomous animals.

Foraging Areas

Correlated with its diverse diet, the foraging areas of the roadrunner are myriad, including open ground, underground, midair, pavement, grass, shrubs, trees, water, and human structures. Animal trails or other open pathways are major roadrunner feeding areas, for these provide room for it to freely walk, run, and maneuver to flush and catch prey. Besides eating insects and other small animals along a trail, roadrunners also pick up insects from the animal dung found there.

Paved roadways are also major foraging areas, probably accounting for the demise of a few roadrunners. Ornithologist James Cornett (2000) observed roadrunners feeding on live grasshoppers on pavement, where these insects did not appear to be as camouflaged as they did on the nearby desert soil. I have often seen the birds feeding on squashed insects and other carrion on pavement.

Foraging roadrunners frequently dig in the ground for food. Desert naturalist Edmund Jaeger (1947) encountered one turning over large plates of caked, dry mud with its bill, looking underneath for insects. In less than ten minutes, this bird had turned over more than thirty of the seven-inch-wide mud plates, finding many insects beneath them. I have watched roadrunners dig with their bills in sandy soil or loose dirt, throwing sand afar, especially when digging in the funneled holes of ant lions.

Sometimes roadrunners forage in trees or bushes rather than on the ground. Amid the foliage and branches they find such delicacies as caterpillars, daddy longlegs, European mantids, bird eggs, and bird nestlings. At one West Texas nest I watched, arboreal feeding was especially common at times when the nearby cottonwood trees were loaded with caterpillars.

Foraging Methods

Because of the many types of food that the roadrunner eats, the bird needs to be a jack-of-all-trades when it comes to techniques for detecting and capturing prey. Its most common foraging mode is a slow walk, interspersed with brief stops while it peers into, under, and on top of everything along its pathway. When it spots prey, the capture happens so quickly that observers get only a partial glimpse of the technique and skill involved. During my field studies, I was often able to follow closely behind foraging roadrunners, for they quickly adjusted to my presence. Even when I was as close as ten feet, however, I never saw the prey before it ended up in the bird's bill.

One clever way that the roadrunner forces prey from its hiding place is to startle it by wing-flashing. Slowly walking or standing still, a roadrunner will quickly thrust its wings outward and then back to its body. As the wings extend outward, the wing feathers are almost fully spread, revealing the white patches near the center of each feather (fig. 6). The sudden movement and the flash of white cause insects and lizards to scurry from hiding places, only to be snapped up by the waiting bird. I have watched wild roadrunners do this in many different habitats. Juvenile roadrunners as young as thirty-five days old wing-flash as they begin to forage for food on their own. My hand-reared birds would flash their wings as they hunted in the short grass in their large outdoor enclosure.

In tall, thick grass, the roadrunner has little room for ground maneuvering or wing-flashing. Here the bird shifts to another foraging mode. Wyman Meinzer (1993) watched a wing-flapping, tail-fanning, leaping technique used by a roadrunner to flush insects in tall grass. Another flushing method the bird uses in tall grass is to brush the grass with its head held low to the ground, forcing insects to move.

Other birds that wing-flash to flush insects—such as the pheasant cuckoo, the northern mockingbird, and the American redstart—also have white patches on their wings (Selander and Hunter 1960; Sieving 1990). However, some birds that wing-flash do not have wing patches, including some tropical American mockingbirds, the gray catbird, and the brown thrasher.

The roadrunner takes every opportunity to let others do the work of flushing or capturing prey for it. Several observers have reported this "lazy" way of getting food. Ornithologists Florence Merriam Bailey (1922, 1923) and Sally Spofford (1978) reported roadrunner attacks on live birds caught in traps. One naturalist endured a roadrunner stealing small

Figure 6. Roadrunner flashing its wings to flush prey.

birds he had shot before he could retrieve them himself (A. B. Howell 1916). A bird bander using mist nets to catch birds unintentionally provided several meals for a roadrunner (Barclay 1977).

In South Texas a roadrunner was seen moving along with a white-tailed deer herd that was feeding in low vegetation (Michael 1967). Closer observation revealed that the roadrunner was grabbing insects stirred up by the deer. This behavior is similar to that of cattle egrets that associate with cows and other large, grazing animals to eat insects found on and around them. The scissor-tailed flycatcher follows wild turkeys and feeds on insects flushed by them.

Roadrunners will even follow humans to find prey. In the mesquite grasslands of South Texas, a common ranching practice is to burn the needles from prickly pear cacti to allow cattle to eat the juicy pads and fruity without getting thorns. One rancher reported that a roadrunner followed the pear-burning worker every day, searching the singed cacti for roasted worms and bugs (Dobie 1939). In farming country, roadrunners will follow a plow to grab insects and worms exposed in the newly turned soil (Dobie 1939).

The roadrunner may wait, catlike, in ambush outside animal holes or near bird feeders until unsuspecting prey appears. A black-chinned hummingbird met its end when a roadrunner caught it in midair at a hummingbird feeder that ornithologist Sally Spofford (1976) was watching. Ornithologist Dale Zimmerman (1970) reported a roadrunner lying in wait in a juniper for house sparrows in an area where they usually congregated. Another observer reported roadrunners catching a house finch and two young California quail by lying in wait at a bird feeder (R. E. Wright 1973).

There are many popular accounts of bird-watchers supplying meat or dog food to their resident roadrunner to the extent that the bird sometimes becomes dependent on this food source. I observed this in New Mexico, where a homemaker daily put out strips of raw chicken for a roadrunner pair that were nesting in a yucca in her yard. The birds would grab the meat as soon as she moved away a few feet. When their eggs hatched, they took the chicken, along with food from the dog dish, to feed the nestlings.

Even in areas far from human influence, roadrunners quickly learn to panhandle. One regularly came to a camp in a New Mexico wilderness area to eat the entrails of small animals that biologists were skinning (F. M. Bailey 1922).

I was amused to hear from an Arizona man whose wife made small meatballs for their resident roadrunner to eat. After the bird began nesting nearby, it took these meatballs, often two at a time, to feed the nestlings. The meatballs disappeared so fast that his wife started freezing them in large quantities to keep ahead of the roadrunner's demands. Soon the bird brought its newly fledged juveniles for the treats. Many people have written me about wild roadrunners regularly coming by their home for a handout.

Killing and Swallowing Large Prey

Unlike birds of prey that use their feet to kill, tear, or handle their prey, roadrunners stun and crush prey only with their bill, and they swallow it whole rather than in pieces. Biologists who have examined roadrunner-killed animals report blows to the base of the skull as the cause of death (Anthony 1896; Bleich 1975).

Landing a snake for dinner, especially a poisonous one, is one of the greatest tests of the fighting skill and mettle of the roadrunner. The bird first slowly circles the snake sideways with tail fanned and tipped toward the snake, then jabs at the snake's head with lightning speed. The bird will often flash its wings rapidly, revealing white patches, as it circles the snake. The northern mockingbird also flashes its wings, showing a white patch, in the presence of snakes (Selander and Hunter 1960).

When the snake strikes back, the faster-moving roadrunner leaps out of reach of the strike, then begins jabbing at the head again. Another maneuver of the roadrunner is to hold its wings fanned outward, like a bullfighter's cape, to divert the snake's strike. The final kill is made by repeated jabs to the snake's head. Sometimes a pair will work together in a team attack, with both circling the snake until one gets an opportunity to jab at the snake's head.

Before swallowing large prey, the roadrunner usually beats it repeatedly on a rock or other hard surface. Lizards, snakes, birds, and small mammals may be beaten for as long as thirty minutes. The research of Beal and Gillam (1979) found that this beating behavior resulted in broken bones and an elongated body, making the prey easier to swallow than an intact body would be. My hand-reared birds would kill and beat the live vertebrate food I gave them. They would even vigorously beat a two-inch-long strip of meat before they swallowed it.

Bird prey receives the additional treatment of feather plucking. Most of the bird's wing and tail feathers are pulled out as the roadrunner holds the end of each feather in its bill and rapidly shakes and beats the bird's body.

Roadrunners require a sturdy tail support for roosting, for they back into a corner or against a tree branch with the tail held vertically upward. Two San Diego roadrunners roosted through a winter, each on a windowsill of a house. These birds must have been in the typical lethargic stupor, for they were not bothered by people or dogs being within inches on the other side of the glass (Abbott 1940).

Predation on roadrunner eggs and nestlings probably accounts for more losses than does predation on adults. Nest predation and the parents' responses to it are discussed in chapter 5.

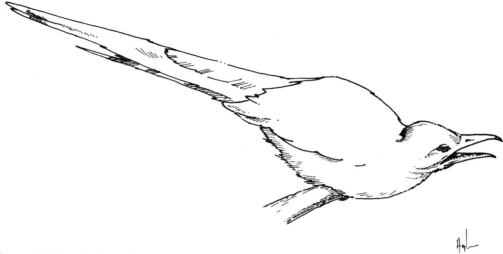

Figure 13. Female giving the whine call from a perch.

bird runs at the other in an attack posture, although physical contact is not made. This posture also occurs in territorial fighting, when one roadrunner invades another's territory.

The Role of the *Coo*

Given that the *coo* is the common call during the breeding season, I examined its role in courtship by playing a *coo* recording to wild birds and observing their reactions. Playing the call alone removes the possibility that the bird is responding to the sight of a visual display made by the calling bird. To my surprise, wild roadrunners responded to a tape of the *coo* not only with calls but also with some of the visual displays of roadrunner courtship.

Nearly 90 percent of the more than two hundred roadrunners tested approached the source of the *coo* call. Nearly half of the birds cooed in response, and another 12 percent barked. About 10 percent of the birds tail-wagged or pranced, though no other roadrunner was present. Six birds approached with a lizard or an insect in their bill as they tail-wagged. Several approached without food, then left the area, soon returning with a lizard or an insect in their bills.

In these *coo* tests I did not know the sex or breeding status of the birds that responded, and some of them could have been unpaired or juvenile. I also played the *coo* tapes to paired wild birds whose sex and phase of breeding I knew. The male responses to the *coo* tape included *coo*ing, prancing, and tail wagging, while the female responses included barking, whining, stick presentation, and sideways and upward tail flicking. All of the male responses increased as the nesting cycle progressed from pre–nest building to the time the nestlings fledged. However, the females were responsive only before and during nest building.

5

Getting Together,
Nest Building, and Incubating

After watching roadrunner parents at several nests, I realized that successful nesting requires not only nesting skills but also efficient coordination of duties between the sexes. The first challenges that potential parents face is to come together as a united pair after foraging separately during the winter. Once together, they must agree on a safe place to build their nest. After egg laying starts, they face a myriad of hardships and irritations, including egg-eating snakes, ants in the nest, and temperature extremes. On top of all this, they are unwelcome neighbors in the local bird community. Other nearby nesting bird species repeatedly dive at roadrunners to keep them away from their own eggs and nestlings, which roadrunners are prone to eat or feed to their own young.

In this chapter and the next we will see how roadrunners overcome the odds to get together, mate, and successfully raise their young. Nesting data, including nest heights, clutch size, and types of nest structures, came from the North American Nest Record Card Program (Cornell Laboratory of Ornithology, n.d.); Arizona nest records (Arizona Game and Fish Breeding Bird Survey, n.d.); and the author's field notes from twelve nests studied in depth and sixteen other nests studied briefly. These nests were in Oklahoma, New Mexico, and West Texas.

Getting Together

In late winter or early spring the first signs of male breeding behavior are frequent *coos* throughout the day. The male appears bent on declaring his intentions throughout his territory, for after cooing for a while in one spot, he moves a few hundred feet away and begins again. Exactly what his intentions are at this time is not clear, for besides the time for courting, this is the time for declaring and defending the breeding territory.

Often a distant roadrunner *coo*s or barks during or immediately after the first bird's *coo* call. Occasionally, two distant birds appear to be exchanging bark calls. Direct encounters with other roadrunners in the area bring forth behavior ranging from intense tail wagging with courtship food to aggressive chases and attacks.

During this time it is difficult to tell territorial behavior from early courtship behavior. One bird will chase the other or vice versa, often for several hours. Fast running is interspersed with low, gliding flights, frequent rest stops, tail wagging, prancing, and cooing. Occasionally, the pursuing bird attacks with its wings spread and its tail raised and fanned.

Most likely these chases are between males, as well as between male and female. Since this attack posture is like that of territorial aggression between males, some chasing may be territorial rather than courtship behavior. During my field observations, I saw actual fights between roadrunners only four times. The drawing at the beginning of this chapter shows two birds in a territorial encounter.

The first sign that the pair is established is when they forage together for most of the day. However, they still roost separately for a few days. Each morning, separated once again, the male's *coo*s and the female's responding barks help them get together for the day. They often exchange calls, especially a soft growl call, as they move in the same general direction. Soon the pair starts roosting close together, often in the same bush or tree.

Nest-building behavior begins with small sticks being passed back and forth between the pair. One member of the pair whines while perched on a branch or other aboveground spot, followed by the other bird searching for a stick to give to it. The whining bird usually drops the stick and begins foraging again. The male will sometimes prance or tail-wag near the female during this time, but mating doesn't occur at first.

Selecting Safe Nest Sites

Soon after the birds start giving sticks to one another, they begin looking for the right nest site, which appears to be a joint effort. The pair may be testing sites as they move together into shrubs, trees, or other high perches. The female often whines as the two perch close together or side by side in a tree or shrub, prompting the male to leave and return with a stick for her. She may begin nest-building motions with the stick or drop it, in which case the pair continue to search for the perfect site. Male courtship displays and female whining occur in the midst of this search. Mating occasionally occurs but is not frequent until the pair begins to build the nest.

We don't know what prompts the birds to choose a particular nesting site, but looking at common features at many nest sites helps define a few of the bird's requirements. I compiled unpublished nesting information from the North American nest card record program (Cornell Laboratory of Ornithology, n.d.) and the Arizona Breeding Bird Atlas (Arizona Game and Fish Department, n.d.), along with published nesting records and my nesting observations.

Plate 1. Adult roadrunner in Chihuahuan Desert of West Texas.

Plate 2. Male roadrunner with crest erect and colored skin patch displayed; captive bird of Oklahoma origin.

Plate 3. Male roadrunner with crest partially erect and colored skin patch displayed; captive bird of Oklahoma origin.

Plate 4. Recently fledged roadrunner, about twenty-five days old; Chihuahuan Desert of West Texas.

Plate 5. Roadrunner starting to swallow Texas horned lizard. Photo provided by Dr. Wade Sherbrooke.

Plate 6. Roadrunner swallowing Texas horned lizard. Photo provided by Dr. Wade Sherbrooke.

Plate 7. Juvenile roadrunner absorbing heat from the sun on the bare black patch on its back.

Plate 8. Roadrunner sunning during the heat of the day. The function of this sunning behavior is not known but possibly is to rid the bird of feather parasites.

Plate 9. Captive male roadrunner holding Chihuahuan spotted whiptail lizard during the tail-wagging display of courtship. Photo provided by Dr. Wade Sherbrooke.

Plate 10. Mating of roadrunners; Chihuahuan Desert of West Texas.

Plate 11. Roadrunner nest with five eggs under attack by bull snake; Chihuahuan Desert of West Texas.

Plate 12. Roadrunner nest with ten eggs, six feet high in a honey mesquite tree in West Texas.

Plate 13. Female roadrunner incubating the ten eggs at the nest shown in plate 12.

Plate. 15. Nesting adult roadrunner attacking a taxidermic roadrunner mount placed near its nest in West Texas.

Plate 14. Coiled western diamondback rattlesnake, with its head hidden under its coil, after an attack by a wild roadrunner.

Plate 16. Roadrunner nest with four chicks, four days old and younger; Chihuahuan Desert of West Texas.

Plate 17. Twenty-five-day-old juvenile in immobile, erect posture in response to nearby human; West Texas.

Plate 18. Month-old juvenile begging for food from its parent.

Plate 19. Head of four-to-five-day-old chick.

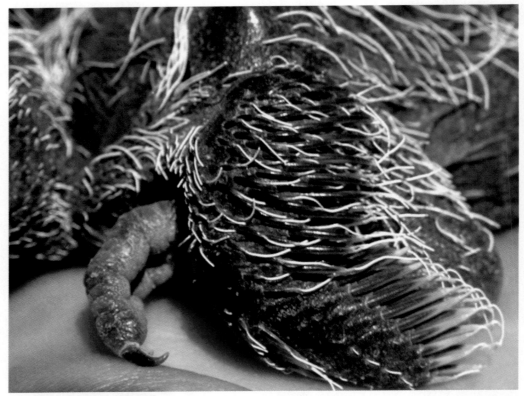

Plate 20. Foot and wing of four-to-five-day-old chick.

Plate 21. Fifteen-day-old roadrunner nestling; Chihuahuan Desert of West Texas.

Plate 22. Twenty-three-day-old juvenile, panting and with drooped wings to allow body heat to escape.

Plate 23. Two-month-old juvenile in West Texas.

Plate 24. Seventy-five-day-old juvenile, with still-blotched juvenile mouth and eye ring of adult.

It appears that the growl of the parent is the major and perhaps only stimulus that causes nestlings to fledge. When I played a tape recording of the growl near nests, older nestlings began moving about the nest or even climbed out of the nest to nearby branches, while younger nestlings gaped for food. At one nest, I was able to lead an older nestling to the ground by playing a tape of the growl call near the nest.

When searching for fledglings in dense vegetation, I would find them by playing the growl tape. I would hear distinctive hollow bill clacking or see the fledgling moving in the brush in response to the sound. Once a wild fledgling ran from its hiding place and jumped on the tape recorder on the ground that was playing the growl call. Standing only a few feet away, I could scarcely believe that this young bird had ventured so close.

Sheltering and Feeding Fledglings

For the first few days after fledging, young birds spend most of their time sitting on low branches or other protective cover, clacking continuously. They are rarely on the ground, except when a parent is nearby. A juvenile is very wary, ceases clacking, and remains motionless when a human is nearby. As a person moves closer to the bird, it freezes in an erect posture with its neck stretched out, bill pointed upward, tail pointed downward, feathers pressed close to the body, and eyes open (plate 17). In this position, it blends in well with surrounding branches. Young black-billed cuckoos assume a similar erect, frozen posture (Herrick 1910; Sutton 1940; Sealy 1985). Sealy noted that this behavior might allow a cuckoo parent to leave the rather helpless young for long periods to seek food for them over a large area.

Parents regularly bring food to fledglings but feed them only about half as much as they do nestlings. Most of the food is now insects rather than reptiles. Several times during the day, a parent leads each fledgling to a new location by slowly walking away, while growling for the chick to follow it to a new hiding place. By the time they have been out of the nest a week, several fledglings usually stay together in or under shelter, waiting for food to come.

After a few days of hiding, fledglings join a parent as it hunts for part of the day. They keep close to the parent, ready to grab food as soon as the parent catches it. At first the fledgling begs like a nestling—crouching with its head drawn into its shoulders, and gaping and buzzing (plate 18).

The young start feeding themselves occasionally when they are about twenty-five days old, although most food is still supplied by the parents. When offering a large food item, a parent drops it on the ground in front of a fledgling, rather than placing the item in the young bird's mouth. This behavior may help the fledgling learn to pick up and beat a large item on its own. Once I saw a parent drop a large lizard (apparently dead) in front of a young bird, pick it up, beat it a few times, then drop it again. The fledgling seemed to get the message, for it picked up and began beating the lizard. Parent and young took turns beating the food for several rounds before the fledgling finally swallowed it.

Fledglings also gain other feeding skills during this time. They begin jumping into the air after butterflies, moths, and other flying insects. As they walk behind or along with a

Figure 14. Thirty-five-day-old juvenile crouching after parental attack (parent in foreground).

parent, they continuously examine the ground, eating items. When about thirty days old, the young may hunt alone or with siblings for part of the day. By this time, a second nest may be occupying the parents for most of the day, so they have little time for the fledglings.

At about this time, parents start vigorously attacking their young whenever they assume a begging posture. Sometimes a parent attacks its juvenile even if it is not begging. When attacked, a juvenile crouches, with head lowered and wobbling, and gives a low whine (fig. 14). The behavior and sound are similar to the whining crouch of the female during nest building.

When about a month old, most fledglings are feeding on their own, primarily eating insects and other arthropods. They may occasionally forage with their parents but do not get much food from them. Adult foraging techniques, including wing-flashing to flush prey, appear in juveniles between thirty and thirty-five days old.

If parents are nesting again, juveniles spend time around the new nest. This may account for some reports of multiple females at a nest. I never saw juveniles from a previous nest help with feeding or other parental duties at their parent's new nest, but I cannot rule this out as a possibility. Juveniles of the groove-billed ani help their parents in their next nest.

I wish I knew how long juveniles stay with their parents. Although adults attacked the older juveniles, the juveniles never left the territory of their parents and never stopped foraging with them completely. My latest field observations were of two-and-a-half-month-old juveniles that were still foraging with their parents for part of the day.

It is likely that juveniles stay near their parents late into their first fall. Groups of three to six roadrunners seen foraging together in early winter could be juveniles with their parents. One biologist observed six roadrunners hunting together until late December (Gander 1958). There are no observations of such groupings in late winter or in early spring, so the family may disband for the winter. Roadrunners are able to breed their first spring (author's observations on captive birds).

Courting While Caring for Fledglings

After all young are fledged, parents forage together again, unless they are incubating eggs or feeding nestlings at a new nest. The male's courtship behavior increases dramatically, with coos, tail wagging, and presentations of food to the female, which may or may not respond. Perhaps the female decides whether renesting will occur, based on some environmental cue, such as food availability or a changing photoperiod. The pair give the growl often, but it is associated more with finding the fledglings than with courtship.

Juvenile birds learn or refine future adult behavior through early experience. Juvenile roadrunners give some calls and displays of adult courtship soon after leaving the nest. These usually appear interspersed with playful chasing of each other, a common juvenile pastime. In this context, I observed wild fledglings cooing, growling, whining, tail-wagging, and offering sticks to one another when the birds were about thirty-five or forty-days old. It is likely that hearing their parents' courtship calls and watching their visual displays encourage fledglings to call and tail-wag.

Without the benefit of a parental example, my captive birds did not give any courtship calls until their first breeding season the next year. One exception barked as a juvenile. Captive juveniles did give visual displays similar to the tail wag, the flick, and the stick offer of the adults. These behaviors were isolated events, rather than part of the pattern of adult courtship.

7

Development of the Young

Even though starting as a half-ounce, helpless lump, a roadrunner will fledge when about nineteen days old and will be almost indistinguishable from its parent by the time it is two months old. The following chapter describes the major milestones in the life of a rapidly growing roadrunner chick.

Hatching

I was elated when Niño's parents, José and Pedra, produced an egg in the typical roadrunner nest they had constructed in their large outdoor enclosure in Norman, Oklahoma. Because they had not incubated any of their previous eggs, I placed this egg in an incubator. I was present when the egg hatched, so I can describe the details of this event.

The first evidence of pipping was a slight crack near the larger end of the egg at 10:00 A.M. on the seventeenth day of incubation. By 8:00 P.M. that night, the crack was about one-sixth-inch long. About an hour and forty-five minutes later, a tiny chunk of shell centered on this crack had been knocked off, revealing the inner membrane of the egg. No further pipping occurred until 6:30 A.M. the next day, when another crack started at the edge of the previous crack. Around 9:00 A.M. the inner membrane in the crack was open, giving a first glimpse of the tiny, black-skinned body inside, which appeared to be heaving regularly. This heaving could have helped the chick saw through the shell with its bill.

The hatching process then moved quickly. By 9:07 A.M. the chick had extended the crack completely around the shell so that one-third of the shell separated from the remainder as the chick pushed and kicked its way out. As the shell separated, the chick's head was visible at the cracked end, with the end piece of shell resting on its head like a beanie. Its small body was still heaving regularly.

Within five minutes the chick was completely out of the shell—a coal black lump with scattered white hairlike strands covering its body. The entire process from making the first faint crack to breaking out of the shell took about twenty-three hours.

After all the effort of hatching, I expected Niño to be exhausted and ready to rest, but immediately the hatchling began scooting about the incubator by pushing its feet and legs to one side and backward, with its tiny head and body supported by the floor of the incubator. Faint grunts and oinks sounded, as the chick made its first moves in its new world. It moved rapidly over a circular area about eight inches in diameter for several minutes, as if searching for something. If it had been in a nest in the wild, it could have easily fallen out of the nest. Its movements stopped whenever I lightly touched its back or covered it with a tissue. In the nest, a hatching chick would be confined beneath the incubating parent's body. My touch may have simulated the presence of the parent's body.

Within the next hour, Niño gaped for food whenever I opened the incubator door. The bright reddish pink mouth, fluttering wings, and persistent buzzing noise told me that the bird was hungry.

Nestlings

The newly hatched chick weighs about one-half ounce and is naked and black-skinned, except for pink skin on the rear mandibles and chin area. The bill, legs, and feet are also black. The white hairlike strands that stand out against the black skin of the hatchling are actually modified down feathers that mark the locations where feathers soon emerge. Birds do not have true hair like that of mammals. These strands cling to the tips of the bird's feathers after it fledges, and their presence is a good way to tell a juvenile from an adult roadrunner. Plate 16 shows four wild nestlings, ranging from one to four days old.

Another distinctive feature of the newly hatched chick is a tiny white bump (egg tooth) near the tip of its upper bill. The egg tooth, typical of a bird hatchling, is used to crack the shell during hatching. It stays on the young roadrunner's bill until it is about twelve days old. The hatchling also has a bare black area behind the eye that becomes the blue, white, and bright orange patch of the adult. Plates 16 and 19 show the egg tooth and bare skin area in nestlings.

The weight of a nestling's legs and feet is about 25 percent of that of an adult's feet and legs, although the nestling's body weight is only about 5 percent of that of an adult. Plate 20 shows the large foot and the small wing of a four-day-old nestling. Despite its large feet, the nestling is not able to stand and walk until it is about eleven or twelve days old. However, on a flat surface it can scoot about by kicking and pushing with its curled-up toes, while resting on its belly and tarsi.

Roadrunners on the edges of urban areas may require only small breeding territories because of the abundance of food. I observed a roadrunner pair foraging over about twenty-one acres in a residential area in New Mexico. During this time, they raised two successful nests. Insects were plentiful on nearby vacant lots, which had native desert scrub vegetation. Adult house sparrows, bird nestlings, bird eggs, and pet food were major food sources for these parents. At another suburban nest I watched, the breeding territory covered about sixty acres.

Influences on Population and Range

The rapid eastward range expansion of the roadrunner during the last century shows the ability of this opportunistic species to take advantage of favorable conditions when they appear. Although this movement could be explained away as simply a matter of time for the species to spread out from its original population center, the speed of the movement is remarkable. Also notable is that, coming from a desert habitat, this bird moved with apparent ease into humid, deciduous eastern woodlands.

During the last hundred years, generations of roadrunners gradually moved across the central plains into the wooded habitats of eastern Kansas, eastern Oklahoma, and East Texas. From there, they continued eastward to the edge of the Mississippi River valley of Missouri, Arkansas, and Louisiana. This roughly five-hundred-mile movement is a remarkable distance for a ground-dwelling species whose individuals move only a few miles during their lifetime.

I think that this unusually fast expansion of the roadrunner population into new eastern areas can be explained as a combination of three factors: the species' long history as a dweller of open woods, rather than desert; the extreme flexibility of the species' habitat, diet, and breeding habits; and human changes in the landscape that enhanced habitats for this species. The following sections discuss these factors as a background for understanding its range expansion.

Prehistoric Roadrunner Habitat

Although in modern times the roadrunner has occurred mainly in desert areas, a look at its history as a species tells a different story. The roadrunner's expansion into colder and wooded eastern areas may not be so remarkable when we consider that the bird's history as a species is a great deal older than that of the southwestern deserts. Comparing the roadrunner with other western U.S. bird species whose lineages go back this far, the roadrunner is one of the few that now covers a larger area of the United States than it occupied in prehistoric times.

The oldest-known fossil of the modern roadrunner, *Geococcyx californianus,* is from a cave in southeastern New Mexico and is estimated to be about 33,500 years old (Harris and Crews 1983). Other roadrunner fossils include twenty-five found in the Rancho La Brea tar pits in Los Angeles County (Howard 1962), several from the Southern California counties of Santa Barbara and Kern (Larson 1930), and several from northern Mexico. Paleontologists have determined that the bones of these fossil roadrunners are no different from those of the modern bird. However, we cannot assume that all aspects of the early roadrunner's behavior and physiology were the same as the roadrunner of today. Fossils of the larger, extinct Conkling's roadrunner are also reported from several southwestern locations and Mexico (see chapter 1).

One of the most remarkable things about roadrunner prehistory is the types of habitat it formerly occupied. Plant fossils show that until about eight thousand years ago, open woodlands covered the areas that today are the desert scrub and desert grassland of the Southwest (Van Devender 1977). Woodland species included juniper, piñon pine, and evergreen oaks. Some shrubs of today's deserts occurred in the woodland as well, including Joshua tree, desert almond, shad scale, and four-wing saltbush. The chuckwalla, the desert tortoise, and other reptiles that today are only found in desert habitats roamed these woods. The climate was cooler and the snow line was lower on western mountains than at present. Pine and spruce forest occurred at higher elevations above these woodlands, with tundra-like conditions on some of the highest mountaintops in New Mexico.

Considering that for two-thirds of its history, the roadrunner was a species of cool, open woodlands rather than of desert scrub, a remarkable adaptation took place thousands of years ago, when its population survived the gradual development of desert scrub and grassland habitats that were emerging on the lowlands of the Southwest as the climate warmed. As a species, it never left its woodland home, however, for it still occurs and nests in open woods on southwestern mountains, especially in oak encinals, pine-oak woodlands, and piñon-juniper woodlands. Even in desert lowlands, roadrunners, like most other "desert" birds, are more common near wooded arroyos and riparian areas than in the midst of spindly, low desert scrub.

Roadrunner Adaptability

In the above discussion, we saw how the roadrunner's history characterizes it as much a bird of open woodlands as of deserts. But this information does not pin down the specific features of the bird that predispose it to a rapid invasion of new areas. To do this, we must glean clues from its everyday life. Just about every aspect of its natural history points to a predisposition to take advantage of new opportunities, as detailed in the following list:

Omnivorous diet, eating everything dead or alive, plant or animal
Typically long breeding season, with up to three clutches per year
Nest site flexibility, allowing the use of any sturdy vegetation or artificial structures
Complex courtship displays, including feeding of the female, which promote stability
throughout the breeding season and may tie nesting to food supply

Given this adaptability, the roadrunner population was ripe for expansion eastward as the landscape at the eastern edge of its range was opened up by human settlement.

Humans and Roadrunner Range Expansion

Although habitat destruction by humans is blamed for much animal extinction, the westward movement of pioneer farmers into the heartland of the United States ironically coincided with and probably facilitated the eastward expansion of the roadrunner through this area. The settlers' modification of the landscape made better roadrunner habitats than had existed there before Euro-American settlement.

The roadrunner's needs are simple—open ground or short grass where it can feed, with tall vegetation nearby where it can roost and nest. If tall vegetation isn't present, then about any aboveground object seems to work. The habitats in which roadrunners do not occur are characterized by one or more of the following features:

Continuous tall grasses with no shrubs, trees, or sturdy cacti
Closed woodlands or forests with a dense understory of brushy vegetation
Desert scrub that is a monoculture of small, spindly shrubs such as creosote bush or sagebrush
Large continuous wetland complexes, such as floodplain forests, wet meadows, and marshes

These habitats do not provide the safety of tall vegetation for nesting and roosting, they lack open areas for foraging and nest location, or they are hard for a ground dweller to traverse.

Some of the changes brought on by settlement that provided the open ground and tall vegetation needed for roadrunner habitat included:

Clearing of the expanses of Great Plains grasslands and prairies in Kansas, Oklahoma, and Texas
Planting trees in grassland areas around homes and along fencerows
Clearing openings in closed-canopy woods in Arkansas, Louisiana, Oklahoma, and East Texas
Providing roadway corridors through tall grass and woods
Elimination of fires and bison, both of which had kept trees and shrubs at bay in the grasslands
Draining wetlands for farming

In addition, the roadrunner tolerates human presence very well, as evidenced by its survival in many suburban areas today (Webster 2000; Cornett 2001).

Range Expansion History

Keeping in mind the factors discussed above, we now will look at the roadrunner's trek across the south-central United States. Figure 16 shows the general areas of this range expansion.

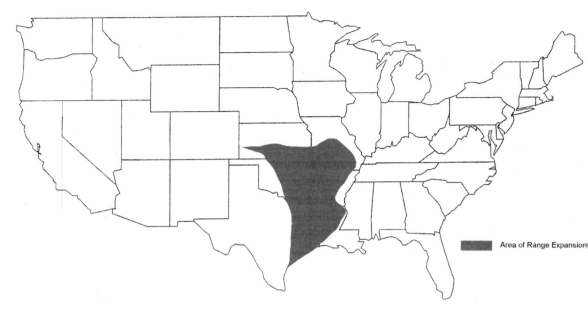

Figure 16. Range expansion of roadrunner from 1900 to 1975.

1830–1900

In 1835 the roadrunner's known range was depicted as extending from the tip of Baja California, Mexico, to the San Francisco area (Ridgway 1916). At that time, most of the interior western United States had not been explored, so the roadrunner's geographic range east of California was unknown. It was not until the 1850s that major U.S. government–sponsored expeditions provided a look at its range. These expeditions surveyed boundaries along the U.S.-Mexican border, explored potential railroad routes, and established wagon routes for pioneers moving westward. Most expeditions included army surgeons, who were often naturalists and compiled information on geology, paleontology, and biology. An interesting historical side note is that Spencer F. Baird, assistant secretary and later director of the Smithsonian Institution was the person who insisted that the surgeons selected for these expeditions also be naturalists.

From these government reports (Baird 1859; Coues 1874; Yarrow, Henshaw, and Cope 1875; Bendire 1895; Ridgway 1916) and the records of the American Ornithologists' Union (1886, 1910), it appears that the roadrunner's *known* distribution prior to 1900 was in nine states:

Arizona—statewide, but uncommon in the north
California—statewide, except in high elevations and the northern tier of counties
Colorado—southeastern, southwestern, and central areas
Kansas—southeastern corner of the state
Nevada— southern area of the state

New Mexico—statewide, but uncommon in the north
Oklahoma—southwestern corner of the state (Indian Territory) and in the panhandle
Texas—in the southeastern, southwestern, and central areas and in the panhandle
Utah—southern areas

In 1853 John Newberry, an army surgeon-geologist for the Pacific Railroad Survey, provided a northernmost U.S. record for the roadrunner from Fort Reading, in Northern California at the upper end of the Sacramento Valley (Newberry 1857). This is still one of the northernmost U.S. records for the species.

The northern edge of the roadrunner's range extended from California through southern Nevada, southern Utah, central Colorado, and southwestern Kansas. The eastern edge of the bird's range stretched from southwestern Kansas, western Oklahoma, and central Texas to the Gulf coast of Texas. The southeasternmost record was from Navarro County in north-central Texas in 1882.

1900–1940

Before the 1900s the eastern edge of the roadrunner's range abutted grasslands and prairies from southwestern Kansas to South Texas. The demise of the buffalo and fire suppression had already allowed woody growth to invade these plains. Ranchers were the first settlers in much of the area, and the grasses were eventually overgrazed. A gradual shift from unfenced ranches to small farms took place as homesteaders came to plow the land. With settlers came roads and tree plantings for windbreaks. Overfarming eventually led to erosion and soil loss, resulting in the dust bowl days of the 1920s and 1930s. As farms were abandoned, more woody vegetation invaded the fields. The plains then provided an ideal habitat for the roadrunner—a mix of open land with shrubs or trees.

In Oklahoma, changes came swiftly after the territory was opened for Euro-American settlement in 1889. Oklahoma ornithologist Margaret Morse Nice (1931, 22–23) wrote of the landscape changes that came with this settlement: "On April 19, 1889, the white man swarmed down on the land, much of whose wild life was still undisturbed. . . . Since then in eastern Oklahoma the primeval forests have been largely cut down, while in western Oklahoma the prairies have been turned into farms, towns, and cities." She listed many grassland birds that quickly declined in number or became extinct in Oklahoma because of these rapid habitat changes. However, she noted that some insect-eating birds of open country benefited by the trees and shrubs in the former prairie areas. She reported the roadrunner to be present in all but the eastern third of the state in the 1920s. Another observer, Walter Colvin (1935), reported a roadrunner sighting in southeastern Oklahoma in 1920. In 1934 a nest was reported as far northeast as Arkansas City in south-central Kansas (Colvin 1935). The first Arkansas record was in 1936 from Hempstead County (southwestern part of the state).

In Texas the blackland prairie, a narrow prairie band that extended from north-central Texas to south-central Texas, was plowed for cotton farming before the Civil War, and its rich soil was depleted before the Great Depression. Landowners converted much of this land to pasture, which was soon invaded by shrubs and trees. My mother grew up on an East Texas cotton farm just east of this prairie belt in the early 1900s and remembers that there were neither trees nor roadrunners on this land when she was young. Around 1930 the land was converted to pasture. Today oak groves dot these pastures, and roadrunners occur there. The first roadrunner record from this area was in 1936.

By 1940 the roadrunner population had extended eastward to south-central Kansas, southwestern Arkansas, and northwestern Louisiana (James and Neal 1986; Lowery 1974). It had also moved northward in western and central Kansas to the Arkansas River.

1940–1980

During the 1940s roadrunners appeared in northwestern Arkansas and in central and south-central parts of the state in the 1950s. In the 1960s this species advanced across the Ozarks to the Mississippi River basin in northeast Arkansas (James and Neal 1986).

Roadrunners were first reported in southeastern and east-central Kansas in the 1950s (Brecheisen 1956). The first Missouri record was in 1956 near Branson in southwest Missouri (Brown 1963).

In the late 1960s roadrunners first occurred in north-central Louisiana (Goertz and Mowbray 1971). The roadrunner advanced eastward across Louisiana, Arkansas, and southern Missouri until about 1975, when it reached its current easternmost boundaries near the Mississippi River basin.

It also advanced northward to the Missouri River in central Missouri by 1975 but later retreated after three severe winters in the late 1970s (Norris and Elder 1982). The range of the Missouri population declined from thirty-six counties in the southern half of the state in 1976 to ten southern counties by 1978. Recently roadrunners have started moving northward again in this state (Robbins and Easterla 1992).

Many parts of the region where Arkansas, Missouri, and Oklahoma meet are dominated by a cedar glade habitat. These glades consist of openings in oak-hickory forests where shortgrass prairie and eastern red cedar grow in rocky terrain that is strewn with boulders. Several other southwestern species reach their northeastern range limits in these glades, such as a collared lizard species (Probasco 1976).

1980 to the Present Time

The only recent confirmed new roadrunner record along its northeastern range boundary is that of a bird that was seen near Lawrence, Kansas (Douglas County), in the 1998–99 winter (Kansas Bird Records Committee 2002). No further roadrunner sightings have been reported from this area. This record and other onetime roadrunner sightings that are out of the bird's normal range probably represent single wanderers rather than a range expansion. Examples of "wanderer" records show up in figure 15, such as those in northern Colorado near the Wyoming border, in northwestern California along the Oregon border, in northern Utah, and in northern Kansas.

Unconfirmed "out-of-range" reports of the roadrunner come from southeastern Iowa (Petersen 1970), western Mississippi in 1982 (Terence Schiefer, Mississippi Bird Records Committee, pers. comm.), southwestern Oregon in 1998 (Oregon Bird Records Committee 2003), and Manitoba, Canada (Koes 1991). The Canada sighting was undoubtedly an escaped captive bird.

Barriers to Further Expansion

Given that the roadrunner's range has not expanded significantly northward nor eastward since the mid-1970s, this roaming species may have reached its limits. It is probable that various combinations of factors have halted the bird's range expansion. As these factors wax or wane over time, the local range can be expected to expand or shrink, as happened in the 1970s in central Missouri. On the other hand, with long-term climatic changes associated with global warming, the roadrunner's northern range boundaries could gradually advance northward in the future.

Taking into consideration the basic needs and survival mechanisms of the roadrunner, we can speculate on what environmental factors along the edge of its range may be at work to limit its advance northward or eastward. Keep in mind that a correlation of a factor with the edge of its range does not necessarily make for a cause-and-effect relationship. The following discussion of possible limiting factors raises as many questions as it answers, but I hope that it will stimulate further research into the roadrunner's ecological relationships.

Rivers, Wetlands, and Bottomlands

In Kansas the roadrunner's northern range roughly coincides with the floodplain of the Arkansas River, although a few stragglers have reached points northward. In Missouri the northernmost records are to the south of the Missouri River (Norris and Elder 1982).

Along the entire eastern range boundary of the roadrunner, an obvious physical barrier to any ground-dwelling bird is the vast Mississippi River basin, including the Mississippi delta in Louisiana. In east-central Arkansas and in Louisiana, the roadrunner's range stops short of this river's floodplains and wetlands. Roadrunners do not occur anywhere in the vast wetlands and bottomlands along Louisiana's entire Gulf coastal area.

Upland areas with open woods in southeastern Missouri appear to be good roadrunner habitat, but no roadrunner sightings have occurred there to date. A study of roadrunner ecology along the eastern and northeastern range boundaries would give us a better understanding of the species' requirements and factors limiting expansion.

Climate

In *Atlas of Wintering North American Birds,* biologist Terry Root (1988) examined the distribution and abundance patterns of North American wintering birds and the relationship of these patterns to environmental factors. She reported that the only factor that correlated with the roadrunner's U.S. range was the number of sunny days. Its range roughly coincides with areas that receive at least 140 sunny days a year (clear days from sunrise to sunset). Other factors—average minimum January temperature, mean length of frost-free days, mean annual precipitation, average annual general humidity (pan evaporation), elevation, and structure of vegetation types—were not coincident with the roadrunner's range. Root did find that the species is most abundant in areas of extremely low humidity (areas where the annual pan evaporation measures more than one hundred inches).

The three factors that were most associated with other bird species' winter range limits were average minimum January temperature, mean length of frost-free period, and vegetation. In addition Root suggested that the northern boundaries of wintering passerine birds (the roadrunner is a nonpasserine) appear to be limited by the energy demands of cold temperatures. The northern boundaries of passerine species seem to coincide with the point where raising their metabolic rate to about 2.5 times their basal rate would allow them to keep warm through the night.

In the following discussion of climate as a limiting factor on the roadrunner's northern range, I suggest that a combination of cloudy days, cold temperatures, prolonged snow cover, lack of woody vegetation, and scarce winter food is what limits the roadrunner's northern range. I suspect that roadrunner populations and range boundaries are in a state of flux wherever the species encounters these conditions, some of which may vary from year to year.

In the northern areas of the roadrunner's range, cold temperatures and many consecutive days below freezing may lead to exposure deaths in roadrunners. Cold weather also causes food shortages and makes it difficult for birds to forage. Stomach contents from roadrunners in winter indicate that they feed on insects, insect egg cases, fruits, berries, and carrion (see chapter 3 for information on the roadrunner's winter diet.)

Several ornithologists have suggested that the roadrunner may enter a torpid state during extreme winter weather and food shortages. Although the roadrunner does become hypothermic on cold nights and possibly on cold, dark days, there is no evidence that it is torpid for long periods (see chapter 3). Thus it must continue feeding to survive.

However, finding food in areas that have prolonged extremely cold temperatures and/or snow cover is another matter. Snow cover not only buries this food but also makes it difficult for a ground-dwelling bird to move about and forage. The only food items that roadrunners have been observed eating during periods of heavy, prolonged snow cover have been other birds, such as sparrows and starlings, and handouts from humans.

Documenting the amount and length of snow cover at the northern edge of the roadrunner's range from year to year would be interesting. In her atlas of wintering birds, Terry Root did not examine snow cover as a factor, because it is so variable and could be locally melted near a log or rock, making a feeding area available to most birds (Terry Root, Stanford University, pers. comm.). However, I think that finding isolated, melted patches in deep snow would be more of a challenge for the roadrunner than it would be for flying birds. During times of snow, I suspect that roadrunners in wooded areas forage primarily in bushes or trees and are more successful in finding food than roadrunners in open areas with only ground vegetation.

Besides being a roadblock in the Midwest, cold temperatures and snow cover may hinder the roadrunner's northern advance in the western states of Colorado, Nevada, Utah, and California. Cold temperatures, snow, and lack of woody vegetation in the four-corners area of Arizona, Utah, Colorado, and New Mexico may explain the low populations or absence of the roadrunner in these areas.

Some areas where roadrunners occur have cold winters, snow cover, and scarce winter food, but these areas also have winter sunshine (at least the 140 sunny days from sunrise to sunset reported by Root 1988). Morning sunning behavior is used by the roadrunner to warm up from its energy-saving nightly temperature drop. On the other hand, midwestern winters are characterized by dark, overcast days, sometimes going for weeks without sun. This lack of sunshine could prevent the roadrunner from becoming warm enough to forage, thereby tipping the energy balance to quickly deplete fat reserves.

The results of a lab study of daily activity patterns of roadrunners suggests another negative feature of cloudy, winter days (Kavanau and Ramos 1970). These roadrunners were less active on overcast days than on sunny days during the June and July study. Dim light and darkness inhibited movement of the birds, and bright light stimulated them. Kavanau and Ramos speculated that the roadrunner's visual system is not suited to dim light.

High Elevations

The roadrunner usually occurs below elevations of about seven thousand feet. High mountain ranges border the roadrunner's range boundaries in the western United States, including the Rocky Mountains in Colorado and northern New Mexico and the Cascades, the Klamath Mountains, and the Sierra Nevada in California and Oregon. The Sierra Madre Oriental, the Sierra Madre Occidental, and the Sierra Madre del Sur also appear to be barriers to roadrunners in Mexico. Most likely, the same climatic factors of low temperatures, snow, and food scarcity, discussed previously, work against roadrunner populations in high elevations.

On the other hand, roadrunners have occasionally been sighted at high elevations in the mountains of Colorado and New Mexico (Sutton 1940; A. M. Bailey and Niedrach 1965). They may forage in these higher areas for several months, as one did at more than eleven thousand feet during the 1956–57 winter in Colorado.

Lack of Nesting and Roosting Habitat

As detailed earlier in this chapter, roadrunners do not occur in areas dominated by spindly, low shrubs, for the birds need a mix of open area with tall, sturdy vegetation for safe nesting and roosting sites. This habitat requirement may partially explain the species' failure to advance very far into the Great Basin Desert areas of Utah and Nevada, which have primarily sparse, low shrubs and cold winters.

On the other hand, this species does not occur in areas where the near-to-ground vegetation is too thick, such as in impenetrable woody thickets. Ornithologist Joe T. Marshall, Jr., found roadrunners in pine woodlands in Sonora, Mexico, but not in this same habitat in adjacent areas of Arizona. He attributed the difference to the open, parklike nature of the Mexican woodlands relative to the thick, woody undergrowth in the Arizona woodlands. In the Arizona areas, fire suppression had allowed the dense undergrowth to persist (J. T. Marshall 1957, 1963).

Urbanization

Although roadrunners often thrive in suburban areas (Webster 2000; Cornett 2001; author's observations), the roadrunner population declines as development overtakes natural features when extensive urbanization occurs. This loss of the roadrunner presence has occurred in California for the San Francisco Bay area, coastal Marin County, Santa Barbara County, and San Diego County (J. M. Hughes 1996a).

Parallel Range Expansion of the Armadillo

A discussion on roadrunner range expansion isn't complete without mentioning the range expansion of the nine-banded armadillo, which moved northward and eastward from the Texas-Mexico border in parallel with the roadrunner movement. The armadillo's expansion coincided with the coming of Euro-American settlers to Texas. Grassland clearing, row-crop farming, prairie fire suppression, decreased hunting, and an invasion of shrubs and trees into former open grasslands are some of the factors thought to favor the armadillo's expansion.

Prior to about 1850 the armadillo was not found north of the Rio Grande in Texas. In 1905, biologist Vernon Bailey reported that it occurred in Texas eastward as far as the Colorado River in central Texas (Davis and Schmidly 1997). By 1914 it was in East Texas (Trinity River) and along the coast to the Louisiana line. By the 1970s the species occurred in Louisiana, Arkansas, and Oklahoma, and more recently has ventured into Kansas and Missouri. Another population, introduced in Florida, has spread westward to the Mississippi River.

Unlike the roadrunner, the armadillo is not adapted to an arid climate and thus has spread no farther west than the eastern parts of the panhandles of Texas and Oklahoma. However, its northern range limits in Kansas and Missouri and its eastern limits at the Mississippi River so closely correlate with the range of the roadrunner that we may question if similar factors affect their ranges.

The armadillo's mainly insectivorous diet, supplemented by very small vertebrates, plant matter, and carrion is reminiscent of that of the roadrunner. A study of armadillo food habits that identified the stomach contents of more than eight hundred armadillos found that 93 percent (by volume) of their food was animal matter, mainly insects and other invertebrates (beetles, termites, ants, caterpillars, earthworms, millipedes, centipedes, and crayfish).

Reptiles, amphibians, and birds' eggs were present, but in very small amounts. Other occasional food included berries, fruits, fungi, and carrion (Davis and Schmidly 1997).

Because the armadillo does not hibernate, is insectivorous, needs to eat daily, has very little body fat, and is not good at conserving heat, cold winter weather and snow cover may limit the armadillo's northern range as much as they limit the northern range of the roadrunner.

9

A Bird of the People

My interest in folklore about the roadrunner began when I came across the following words of J. Frank Dobie in his classic article "The Roadrunner in Fact and Folk-lore": "Perhaps no other bird of North America, excepting the eagle and the turkey, which the Aztecs had domesticated long before Columbus sailed, has been so closely associated with the native races of this continent" (1939, 4). Descriptions of roadrunner cures, superstitions, and folktales compiled from his years of studying southwestern folklore fill this fascinating article.

It is not surprising that Native cultures existing side by side with the roadrunner for many centuries have incorporated the bird into many of their folkways and rituals. The roadrunner also was a favorite animal of the early Euro-American pioneers who settled in the Southwest. Western writer Arch Napier (1969), in an article entitled "The Clown That Met the Wagon Trains," described how the roadrunner's antics helped lift the spirits of these apprehensive newcomers to the desert. In her 1922 book on the birds of New Mexico, ornithologist Florence Merriam Bailey told how roadrunners would dart onto roads and race horses, keeping ahead of their trotting.

The roadrunner remains a southwestern icon today, continuing this age-old association with humans. After exploring roadrunner folklore, I came to agree with Dobie that "any animal is interesting to man not only for the facts about him but for what human beings associated with the animal have taken to be the facts" (1939, 19). So I include this chapter on roadrunner folklore to complement the chapters of roadrunner facts.

Pueblo Indian Folklore

Many American Indian tribes of the Southwest knew the roadrunner and incorporated it into their culture. Folklore about this bird is best documented for the Pueblo Indians of northeastern Arizona (Hopi), of northwestern New Mexico (Zuni), and along the Rio Grande drainage in north-central New Mexico (nineteen pueblos, such as Acoma, Cochiti, Nambé, San Juan, Taos, and Sia [Zia]). The Pueblo people have lived in this region for many centuries. Clustered in small villages (pueblos), their society is based on communal farming and worship (Trimble 1993). Before the Spanish invasion, more than one hundred villages were scattered throughout New Mexico. In the Pueblo culture the powers of the roadrunner center around its courage, strength, and endurance, as well as its X-shaped track, thought to have power to confuse the enemy.

Anthropologist Hamilton Tyler described specific historic uses of birds by Pueblo Indians in his 1979 book, *Pueblo Birds and Myths*. Grouping birds by their roles in religion, he placed the roadrunner in the "birds of war" group, along with nuthatches, wrens, woodpeckers, and jays. In the Pueblo context, conflicts with witches and ghosts of the dead are also considered war. Anthropologist and Zuni Ed Ladd documented the uses of birds specifically by the Zuni Pueblo in his 1963 master's thesis entitled "Zuni Ethno-ornithology." These two references are the main sources for the following discussion of Pueblo Indians.

Roadrunner Bravery

The roadrunner's bouts with rattlesnakes give the bird a reputation for bravery, explaining its use in ceremonies devoted to strength and knowledge. The rites of the Little Fire curing society at Zuni involve two persons representing the roadrunner, who hop and skip to the altar with an eagle's wing feather in each hand. The Zuni curing society that treats rheumatic troubles and convulsions is always directed by a member of the Roadrunner Clan.

Roadrunner feathers were used for courage in the scalp ceremony of the Zuni Pueblo (Parsons 1924). The scalp-kickers wore crossed roadrunner feathers in their moccasins and prayer feathers of the roadrunner in their hair. Anthropologist M. C. Stevenson described these scalp-kickers firsthand in 1904 (583–84):

> They wear their ordinary dress, with white blankets bordered in red and blue over their shoulders. The quill ends of two feathers of the chaparral cock—one an upper tail feather and the other an under tail feather—have been crossed and placed in line by their brothers in consanguinity between the second and middle toes of the left foot, the tips of the plumes pointing toward the foot, and the moccasins carefully drawn over. "The feathers give courage, for knowledge and courage come from this bird, who is the keeper of courage." After the girls reach the scene, the same brothers tie similar but somewhat larger feathers to the left side of the head with a strand of the hair and a cotton string already attached to the plumes. The plumes must not be removed for four days.

Roadrunner Swiftness

Roadrunner swiftness is celebrated by the Pueblo Indians. Near the Sia Pueblo in New Mexico, the people run races around a mountain named after the roadrunner. At Hopi in northeastern Arizona, roadrunner feathers are sometimes tied to a horse's tail for speed and endurance. Young Hopi men occasionally eat roadrunners to gain swiftness and endurance. Eating roadrunners to enhance running skills is also reported from the Tarahumara Indians of the state of Chihuahua, Mexico, famous for their long-distance running ability (Dobie 1939).

Roadrunner as Bringer of Rain

Roadrunners are associated with prayers for rain in several Pueblo groups. The roadrunner kachina of the Hopi, called Hospoa, appears in only a few Hopi ceremonies, where it is associated with soliciting rain. One ceremony that always includes Hospoa, along with many other birds, is the Powamu, a bean dance or bean-planting ceremony (B. Wright 1977). Ethnologist Jesse Walter Fewkes described the roadrunner kachina in 1903 (98):

> Hospoa, the Road Runner . . . has a green helmet covered with rows of black and white crescents, a short beak, and stellate eyes. On the back this bird has a painted skin stretched over a framework, called a moisture tablet. To each upper corner are attached two feathers, which project horizontally, and along the edges is a string with attached horsehair stained red. There is a flute in one hand, a rattle in the other. The garments are a ceremonial kilt, girdle, and embroidered sash.

The Zunis of New Mexico use feathers from seventy-two bird species on various types of prayer sticks (Ladd 1963). Specific feathers from different parts of a bird's body may have different meanings. Each member of the tribe offers many prayer sticks during the year. Feathers from some species are used only on the prayer sticks of the spiritual leaders. These include roadrunner feathers, which are reserved only for the prayer sticks of the rain priests (Ladd 1963).

It is noteworthy that in many cultures worldwide, various cuckoo species are associated with predicting or bringing rain and are called "rain bird" or "rain crow" (Ingersoll 1923). In the southern United States, yellow-billed and black-billed cuckoos are often referred to as rain crows.

Roadrunner Tracks for Protection

Pueblos value the roadrunner's X-shaped track because it appears to be heading in opposite directions at once (fig. 17). A Hopi man told anthropologist Polly Schaafsma (1989) that the roadrunner is a liar, because of its tracks.

Drawings of roadrunner tracks are used to ward off spirits of the dead by confusing them as they look for the way to the village. Tracks also protect people from the dead, who

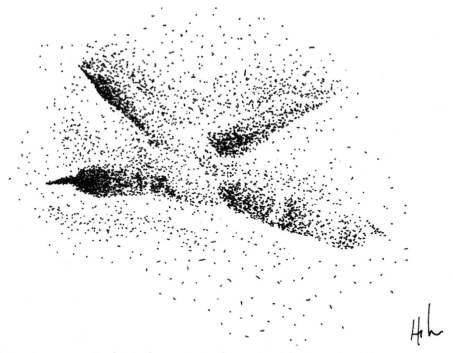

Figure 17. Roadrunner track of right foot, pointing forward and facing to the right.

return on All Souls' Day. Anthropologist Elsie Clews Parsons (1939, 859) gave the following description on All Souls' Day at Nambé: "Before leaving the house each had taken a piece of charcoal and outside had marked on his left sole and on his left palm the cross-like track of the chaparral cock, so that the dead would not make him sick or do him any harm. The chaparral cock has power (*piñan*)."

Roadrunner tracks also protect the dead from evil spirits and witches. At the pueblo of Cochiti in New Mexico, relatives scratched the roadrunner track's X shape into the floor to encircle the body of the deceased (Dumarest 1919), providing "a magic circle for the purpose of preventing evil spirits or Brujos from finding out where the soul of the deceased goes," thus protecting "that soul from their persecutions" (from unpublished 1888 journal of anthropologist Adolph Bandelier, quoted by Lange 1959, 416). Anthropologists Elsie Clews Parsons (1929) and Ruth Benedict (1935) described a ceremony at San Juan Pueblo in which roadrunner tracks were used to protect the altar during the installation ceremony of the winter chief. The tracks were drawn in the meal "road" (a trail of cornmeal). Roadrunner tracks were also painted on the altar wall at the winter chief installation ceremony at Tesuque Pueblo (Parsons 1929).

In several of the New Mexico Pueblo groups, crossed pieces of yucca were laid as stepping-marks on an "altar" road to represent the X shape of roadrunner tracks. Their purpose was to confuse any witch that was pursuing a person (Parsons 1939).

Other Symbolic Uses in Pueblo Culture

The personal fetish represents its owner and is made by a society father and given to a new member on initiation into the society. Roadrunner feathers are used in personal fetishes by the Pueblo Indians at Acoma and Sia (Zia) in New Mexico.

Many Pueblo rituals and ceremonies use birds to represent six directions: north, south, east, west, zenith (above), and nadir (below). Roadrunner feathers represent the nadir in Hopi and Sia ceremonies (Tyler 1979).

Prehistoric Pueblo Indian Culture

Roadrunners have been part of the Pueblo religious expression for more than eight hundred years. Modern-day Pueblo peoples are considered to be descendants of prehistoric Pueblo people (Anasazi, or ancient ones), who were once widespread in the Southwest. The roadrunner and other birds appear to have been at least as important, if not more so, in Anasazi religious expression as they are in the culture of their Pueblo descendants. Although the Anasazi did not have a written language, they left many clues about their culture in their murals and prolific rock art, which give us a glimpse into their ceremonial uses of roadrunners.

Pottery Mound was a Pueblo community in central New Mexico that thrived from about A.D. 1300 to 1475. Mural frescoes from the walls of seventeen excavated kivas (underground ceremonial rooms) are outstanding remains of prehistoric Anasazi art. The artifacts indicate Pottery Mound was a ceremonial center and a significant sacred site. Major features include a Mexican-style pyramid and many prehistoric murals. Bird feathers are the most common single motif in these murals. Feathers of seventeen bird species have been identified. Of these, the roadrunner was the fourth most common species represented, after the bald eagle, the raven, and the yellow-headed blackbird (Hibben 1975).

The Anasazi also left roadrunner characters in their prolific rock art. Another nearby culture—the Mogollon peoples in southern New Mexico and adjacent areas of Texas—used the roadrunner track as a major symbol in its rock art. A few of these sites also have petroglyphs showing the entire roadrunner.

Anthropologist and artist Polly Schaafsma (1989) investigated the use of roadrunner tracks in the rock art and ritual of this prehistoric period. In her interesting article "Supper or Symbol: Roadrunner Tracks in Southwest Art and Ritual," she rejected previous interpretations of these tracks as merely being symbolic for obtaining food. She presents evidence that the roadrunner and/or its tracks had significant religious symbolism in these prehistoric southwestern cultures.

Schaafsma found that roadrunner tracks were associated most often with carnivore tracks, especially those of the mountain lion. Besides appearing in rock art, the tracks of these two creatures are often together on other artifacts from the period. Figure 18 shows one of these petroglyphs from the San Diego Mountains of southern New Mexico. Gleaning

Figure 18. American Indian petroglyph of mountain lion track and roadrunner track near Hatch, New Mexico. Photo by Curtis Schaafsma, provided by Polly Schaafsma.

clues from the modern Pueblo symbolic uses of roadrunners, Schaafsma concluded that the rock art tracks probably were important symbols of the bird's courage and strength. The mountain lion often acts as a guardian and protector for war, hunting, and medicine societies. The occurrence of roadrunner tracks with mountain lion tracks may be an indication that roadrunner tracks also had guardian and protective functions.

Roadrunner bones have been reported from prehistoric Indian ruins at Snaketown (near Phoenix, Arizona), dating from as early as A.D. 100. They appear at a number of later sites, including Grasshopper Pueblo, Wupatki, Tonto Cliff Dwellings, and the University Indian Ruin in Arizona; Gran Quivira, Pueblo Largo, Gila Cliff Dwellings, and Las Madres Pueblo in New Mexico; and Casas Grande in Chihuahua, Mexico (Longacre, Holbrook, and Graves 1982). Archaeologists are not sure of the significance of roadrunner bones at these sites, other than as a source of feathers for rituals and ceremonies.

Other American Indian Folklore

Stories about the roadrunner are preserved in the oral traditions of other southwestern tribes, with some appearing in written form. An Apache story tells why the roadrunner is the leader of the birds. After eliminating several other birds for various reasons, the birds chose the roadrunner because it would be fast in running to meetings and it had good talking ability.

The Pima Indians have a story telling how the orange color on the bare skin behind the bird's eye developed (Curtin 1949). In one version the roadrunner flies to the sun, a four-day trip, to obtain fire for an old woman who wanted to cremate her pet rattlesnake. Lightning struck the head of the roadrunner on the return trip, producing the orange color. In the other version, Lightning Man wounds each side of the roadrunner's head with gunshots.

Mexican Folklore

I was able to explore Mexican folklore firsthand in the state of Chihuahua, Mexico, in the late 1970s. At that time folklorists considered the whole area of northeastern Chihuahua (south of Presidio, Texas, in the Big Bend area of Texas) to be an excellent place to investigate Mexican folk customs. Because of its isolation and lack of outside influences, its residents retained more of the old folklore than did more modern areas of Mexico. Likewise, this area of the Texas border is remote from large urban areas, having only the small towns of Presidio and Redford.

At the suggestion of folklorist Joe Graham at the Institute of Texan Cultures in San Antonio, Texas, I visited the Texas border area with historian Enrique Madrid, Jr., from Redford as my guide and interpreter. Besides interviewing three *curanderos* (male folk healers) and one *curandera* (female folk healer), we also talked with five elderly Mexican men and women in the town of Ojinaga, Chihuahua, Mexico. Later I interviewed several elderly residents of another small Chihuahuan village, Santa Elena.

These people appeared to have firsthand knowledge of the roadrunner in the wild, for they gave accurate answers to my questions on the natural history of the bird. When I played tapes of several common roadrunner calls, they were often able to tell me the context of each call. The following translation of a story written for me by an elderly Mexican man typifies the insightful observation of a person who has lived alongside the roadrunner.

> The Paisano
>
> It's from the country. It eats lizards. It runs along roads. They look for food to keep their offspring fed. The paisano never rests. It spends all its time running along roads. It never rests all day long. El paisano is very healing. It is good for many illnesses. The meat of the paisano is very good and also the lard for sickness. I was sick and the healer prescribed this type of animal for me and I ground the paisano meat up very fine. This animal is very good for healing because it eats snakes and also seeds of wild herbs. The paisano likes very much to make its little house atop the mesquite so no one can bother its young. Here this story of the paisano ends.
>
> Written by Jacinto Hernandes Garsia, Santa Elena, Chihuahua, Mexico

In the following paragraphs I summarize some of the folk-healing uses of the roadrunner. Folk sayings and tales I heard along the way are also included.

A Potent Remedy

The most common healing use described by the curanderos and laypeople alike was for healing skin problems, such as sores, boils, itching, hives, rashes, and stings. Eating a stew or soup made of whole roadrunner boiled with onions, garlic, tomato, cumin, and cilantro was the common prescription. Eating the roasted meat and rubbing lard of the bird on the skin were alternative treatments. One of the men claimed that eating three nestling roadrunners once cured his boils.

Tuberculosis and other lung problems were thought to be cured with roadrunner stew. Two of the curanderos were firm about this cure, although their recipes differed. One insisted that rice must also be an ingredient. Another curandero used fresh roadrunner blood rubbed on the chest for lung problems.

A roasted roadrunner was used as a blood tonic by the curanderos. A variation was to dry the roasted meat and grind it into a powder for sprinkling on food. One woman from Palomas, Mexico, stressed that roasted runner was especially good for anemic children with no appetite. In northern Mexico in the 1920s, West Texas photographer W. D. Smithers (n.d., 38) witnessed the roasting of a roadrunner by a curandero for use as a blood tonic:

> The bird was prepared by killing it without losing any of its blood, then it was taken to the river bank and completely covered with wet clay all over the feathers. In a hole dug in the center of a large fire the clay-covered bird was put in, covered with hot ashes and fire, to cook for about one hour. When removed from the fire, the baked clay was taken off in pieces and the feathers came off with the clay. The meat looked very appetizing, but the thought of it being cooked without being dressed spoiled the desire to try it. The entire bird was the prescription for the cure.

Several laypeople used roadrunner lard as an ointment for earaches, but none of the curanderos used it. One man described how he had rubbed the lard in his hair as a cure for lice but ended up with even more lice. To cure a mental illness called susto, a tea is made from boiling roadrunner tail feathers. The feathers also make good throat swabs, according to one healer.

When asked why the roadrunner is good for healing, all the healers told me that its ability to eat and digest venomous snakes, scorpions, centipedes, tarantulas, and other dangerous creatures is the source of its healing power. The laypeople likewise attributed the roadrunner's healing power to its ability to eat venomous animals. One of the curanderos had two additional reasons for its power—its ability to live a long time without water and a unique digestive organ that it has.

Because the roadrunner fights rattlesnakes and survives, it is thought to know a remedy for snakebite. Several similar tales relate how a roadrunner will pluck and eat the leaves of a certain plant after being bitten by a rattlesnake. Unfortunately, my translator was not familiar with the Spanish name for the plant, and it couldn't be identified.

The curanderos all stressed that the roadrunner is a potent cure and that only one bird is needed, which is fortunate for the roadrunner population. Since none of these healers had roadrunners or roadrunner parts on hand to show us and had other remedies for these same ailments, I asked how common its use really was. The curanderos said they did not catch a bird until they needed it. A young Ojinaga pharmacist expressed a skeptical view of these roadrunner folk cures. He commented that those who can catch a roadrunner don't need a cure.

Roadrunners as Pets and Food

Years ago roadrunners were occasionally kept as pets in Mexican homes. Like a barnyard cat, pet roadrunners would keep homes free from mice, insects, scorpions, and other undesirable pests. They also were kept on hand for healing, as the need arose. In a 1865 article on the birds of South Texas, ornithologist H. E. Dresser wrote: "The Mexicans often keep this bird in a semi-domesticated state, in order to kill them in case of sickness: for they firmly believe that their flesh is a certain cure for many disorders" (1865, 467). People whom I interviewed on both sides of the Rio Grande border said that roadrunners are not kept as pets today.

Two Mexican people said that they ate roadrunners for food, but only rarely. One said that even though it doesn't look appetizing, it is very tasty. John Newberry, a surgeon-geologist with a U.S. government railroad survey, reported in 1857 that the roadrunner was a food item in California: "It is frequently brought into the San Francisco market and is reported very good eating" (1857, 91).

Sayings and Superstitions

A common saying along the border referred to the bill-clacking sound of the roadrunner. I heard several versions of this saying from people on both sides of the border: "No hay para que tonar el pico," which meant "There is no reason to get excited." Literally, this version translates as "There is no reason to snap your bill." Another version is "Ya basta, vete a tonar el pico," which translates as "Enough, go clack your bill somewhere else." The latter is used to get rid of bothersome children. A short version is "No trina el pico," or "Don't get so excited"; the literal translation is "Don't rattle your bill."

Fittingly, the most common superstitions I heard were tied to roads or trails. If a roadrunner crosses in front of you on the road, you will have a bad trip or bad luck in general; if the bird turns back when partway across, you will have a good trip or good luck. If you are following a roadrunner on a road or a trail and it leaves the path, bad luck will follow. J. F. Dobie (1939) reported a different version of this superstition from Indians in Mexico: the roadrunner brings good luck if it crosses the road from left to right, but bad luck if from right to left.

One of the elderly Mexican men I interviewed had spent years as a goatherd and a soldier in very remote parts of Michoacán in southwestern Mexico. This ninety-year-old man told me that because the roadrunner travels all the paths, it will lead you to a lost person. His parents told him a story about a roadrunner leading them to a place in the desert where the body of a missing man was found. J. Frank Dobie (1939) reported another version of this superstition from Mexico: if you are lost, find a roadrunner and follow it, and it will lead you to a trail.

One of the curanderos used some of the roadrunner's behavior for weather forecasting: when a roadrunner is seen stocking up on food in the fall, a bad winter is coming; when the bird calls from a high perch early in the morning, it will rain that day. This reminded me that the clucking call of the yellow-billed cuckoo is also thought to forecast rain, and one of its folk names is "rain crow." (Note: There is no field evidence of roadrunners storing food.)

Stories about the Roadrunner

Most of the folk stories about the bird probably started with an observation of it doing something unusual that became greatly embellished over the years, for there is a grain of truth in many of the stories. In times past, these tales were widespread throughout the Southwest and Mexico, not only among Mexicans and Mexican Americans but also among the Euro-Americans who lived alongside them. We will look at a few of these stories.

A Peculiar Hybrid

With a mischievous twinkle in her eye, an elderly Hispanic woman from a ranch near Redford told me: "Roadrunners are sort of rascals because they do mess around with chickens." That male roadrunners mate with domestic hens appeared to be common knowledge among the people I met along the border. Most described the offspring as a small chicken with a large crest. One man said that the chicks were more paisano (roadrunner) than *gallina* (hen). J. F. Dobie (1939) reported tales of a similar cross between a roadrunner and a game chicken to produce a superior fighting cock.

This folktale probably started because roadrunners often mix with chickens in their pens. Roadrunners have even been reported roosting in sheds with chickens. However, roadrunners are there not to court the chickens but to feed on the many insects that thrive in chicken pens (Jensen 1923).

Reverent Roadrunner

Ornithologist Harry Oberholser (1974) related that some Mexican people in Texas believed the roadrunner to be a Christian because of the X shape of its tracks, which resemble a cross. Others believed it to be a Christian because it bows its head to pray every day (Dobie 1939). The head-bowing posture of the male roadrunner during its *coo* (see fig. 7) or tail-wag display (see fig. 9b) could have started this tale, or possibly one of the bird's sunning positions, which it holds for many minutes as if in a trance, is the origin of the tale (plate 8).

Roadrunner Rancher

Many lizards escape from predators by losing their tail in the jaws or bills of their captors, but the lizards soon grow new tails. A popular story depicts roadrunners keeping herds of lizards for food. Instead of eating the whole lizard, the roadrunner eats just the tail, ensuring a steady supply of tails for itself and its family.

Corral of Thorns

The story of the corral of thorns is probably the most often told and most often debated roadrunner folktale of all time. This tale is found in Mexican, Hispanic, American Indian, and Western folklore, both in the United States and in Mexico (Lewis 1897; Dobie 1939, 1978). The basic story is of a roadrunner that comes upon a sleeping rattlesnake. The road-runner builds a corral of cactus joints around the still-sleeping snake. The bird then begins pecking at the snake to waken it. To escape the roadrunner's attack, the snake frantically thrashes about, striking itself on the cactus spines. The snake eventually dies either from being pierced by the spines, from blows of the roadrunner's bill, or from biting itself in frustration. One version has the roadrunner using a cactus pad like a bullfighter's cape to lure the snake into piercing itself on the spines.

From articles I read about this tale in several bird journals in the late 1880s, it appears that there actually was a scientific debate over the truth of this story. Naturalist C. R. Orcutt, writing in the *West American Scientist* in 1886, claimed to be removing all further doubt about the truth of the story by quoting an eyewitness to "the novel affair." A writer in the bird journal *Avifauna* chided Spencer Fullerton Baird, secretary of the Smithsonian Institution, for perpetuating the story as fact in an article for *Harper's Magazine* (Van Dyke, n.d.).

I can confirm that roadrunners will attack small rattlesnakes for food and large rattlesnakes that are near a nest (see chapter 5). However, these attacks occur in reverse order from that in the thorn corral tale. Instead of being asleep at the beginning of the tale, the snake was "sleeping" in a coil after the roadrunner attack (plate 14 and the drawing at the opening of this chapter). I wonder if someone who came upon a roadrunner standing beside such a coiled snake would think that the snake was sleeping and the roadrunner was going to build a corral. Several of the eyewitness accounts retold by Dobie describe the snake being coiled as it slept.

Names for the Roadrunner

The Spanish explorers who entered Mexico and the southwestern United States were the first Euro-Americans to see roadrunners. One of their names for it was "faisán real," or "royal pheasant." This and other Spanish names for the roadrunner are commonly used in the southwestern United States and Mexico today. Probably the two most commonly used Spanish names in the southwestern United States are "corre camino" ("it runs the road") and "paisano" ("fellow countryman"). In the late 1880s and early 1900s the name "chaparral cock" appeared in most natural history writings about the roadrunner in English. This name persists today in some southwestern areas. Table 5 lists some of the colloquial names for the roadrunner.

The Roadrunner in Modern Culture

Southwestern Icon

The roadrunner continues to be a favorite bird and icon of the Southwest. It is the state bird of New Mexico and the emblem of the Texas Folklore Society. The roadrunner appeared often in popular articles by explorers, naturalists, and pioneers long before the animated version came along. This 1915 depiction of the roadrunner by naturalist D. I. Shepardson is a good example: "No picture of the desert is complete without him. Given a giant cactus, a rattlesnake, a lone cowpuncher and a Road-runner: and your short-story novelist has ample material for an absorbing romance of the plains" (1915, 158).

Early descriptions of the roadrunner often included a humorous story or two about the bird, even coming from serious ornithologists, such as naturalist J. L. Sloanaker. In 1913 he wrote in the *Wilson Bulletin*, a bird journal: "Of all the birds on our list the Roadrunner is doubtless the most unique; indeed, he is *queer*, and would certainly take first prize in the freak class at the Arizona state fair" (Sloanaker 1913, 191). In 1940 ornithologist George Miksch Sutton wrote: "So odd, so even *funny* a creature is the roadrunner that it is natural to caricature him a bit in describing him" (1940, 37).

Animation of the Roadrunner

Since its appearance in the 1950s, the Warner Brothers' roadrunner and coyote cartoon characters undoubtedly have added greatly to the bird's popularity and use as a logo in modern culture. Fondness for the animated character sparks a genuine curiosity about the real bird, which I have used to good advantage to help introduce the real bird to U.S. audiences over the last thirty years. Most people, unfamiliar with the real bird, want a comparison with the animation: Does it go "Beep! Beep!"? Does it really run only on the road? Do coyotes really chase roadrunners? How fast can they really run?

I think the roadrunner's comic reputation comes from its ungainly movements and the situations where its curiosity and boldness lead it. Indeed, there are even a few similarities between the real bird and the animation. The late great character animation film director Chuck Jones captured some of the habits of the real bird and its quirky, gutsy personality very well, and he also put a little of the roadrunner personality into the coyote character.

Curious about the origin of the animated version, I interviewed Chuck Jones under the sponsorship of the National Geographic Society for an article about the roadrunner for

TABLE 5
Common names for the roadrunner

Type of common name	Common name
English names in the Southwest and Mexico	chaparral cock, chaparral, cock-of-the-desert, ground-cuckoo, running cuckoo, racer, lizard bird, snake bird, snake-killer, war-bird, medicine bird, large roadrunner
Spanish names in the Southwest and Mexico	*el correo del camino*—the runner of the road or path; *correr del paisano*—messenger of his countryman; *el paisano*—compatriot or fellow countryman or peasant; *la churrea* or *churea* or *churca*—an imitation of its call; *corre camino*—it runs the road; *tacó*—bite, snack, or heel of a shoe (from *taconar*—to click one's heels, to walk hard on one's heels); *arriero*—(from *arriesgar*—to risk or dare); *faisán real*—royal pheasant
Guanajuato, Mexico	*faisán*—pheasant
Michoacán, Mexico	*faisán mexicano*—Mexican pheasant
American Indian	
Cochiti Pueblo (N.Mex.)	*sha-shua*
Zuni Pueblo (N.Mex.)	*poyyi*
Sia Pueblo (N.Mex.)	*djáck´*
Santa Ana, Cochiti Laguna, Santa Domingo, and San Felipe Pueblos (N. Mex.)	*cá ck´*
Pima (southern Ariz.)	*d'adai*
Paiute (southern Nev.)	*soonung´wuvee toowuv*
Cahuilla (southeastern Calif.)	*puuis*
San Carlos Apache	*góshdiyé*
Shoshone Luiseño	*pooepooe*

Sources: Simmons 1925; Dobie 1939; Lange 1959; Ladd 1963; Birkenstein and Tomlinson 1981; White 1986; Cornett 2001; Machula, n.d.

National Geographic magazine (Whitson 1983). I was pleased to learn that he based his caricature on his memories of roadrunners from when he was a lad in Southern California. He expressed a real affection for the bird, and we had quite an enjoyable time answering each other's questions about our versions of the bird. Details of the creation and characteristics of the animated roadrunner appear in his delightful book *Chuck Amuck* (Jones 1999).

The cartoon establishes the invincible nature of the roadrunner against the coyote, more by the coyote's own ineptitude than by anything the roadrunner does. Ironically, this theme appears in a common folk story about the roadrunner—the corral of thorns, described earlier in this chapter. In this tale the roadrunner taunts the rattlesnake to kill itself through its own foolishness.

Symbol of Speed

The roadrunner is often used as a logo when a business wants to convey speed. Throughout the Southwest there are gas stations, truck stops, truck lines, bus companies, courier services, motels, restaurants, gift shops, and myriad other travel-related businesses that use the roadrunner as their symbol. Probably the most famous use as a speed symbol was by the auto manufacturer Plymouth, when it produced the Plymouth Roadrunner, a 1960s sports car.

While maintaining captive roadrunners in Norman, Oklahoma, for my behavioral studies in the 1960s, I was approached by the local Plymouth dealer, who thought I should be thrilled to let him use my captive roadrunners in a television commercial promoting the car. Naturally, I was not interested in exposing my research animals to the trauma of a television studio. However, Dr. George Miksch Sutton graciously allowed the dealer to use one of the stuffed mounts from the Bird Range at the University of Oklahoma.

As an icon for speed, the roadrunner has also been adopted as a logo by computer services, recording companies, running clubs, motorcycle clubs, hockey teams, and public schools' sports teams, to name a few. During the Vietnam War, it was reported to be one of the favorite insignias of the U.S. soldier.

Popularity With People

Were there no folklore, healing uses, cartoons, or other cultural forces at work to call attention to the roadrunner, it would still be popular with people because of its curious nature and its ready tameness. Wild roadrunners living near homes, ranches, and campgrounds are often approachable, taking food and water put out for them. There are many popular accounts of roadrunners regularly coming by a house for a handout and nesting or roosting on a window ledge or in a garage.

All of this tolerance of human activity has probably helped the range expansion of the species, along with the habitat changes that we humans make in its favor (see chapter 8). The roadrunner's tameness and curiosity provide people with a chance to get to know and love this bird. And roadrunners have provided many a humorous moment for us, such as when they fight their own reflection in a glass door or a hubcap; tease a pet dog or cat; or run-glide in front of our car, as if to taunt us.

Even scientists studying the roadrunner can lose their objectivity and become quite fond of this bird. One of the first to study wild roadrunners was noted ornithologist and bird artist George Miksch Sutton. He began studying the species when only a boy of fifteen and kept several of the birds as pets (Sutton 1922). While still a teenager, he published several articles in bird journals on roadrunner behavior, as well as a drawing of one of his pets (Sutton 1913, 1915). He passed on his lifelong enthusiasm and fondness for this bird to me when I studied ornithology with him at the University of Oklahoma.

In the wake of an article I wrote on the roadrunner for *National Geographic* magazine, I received many letters from readers who wrote about their "pet" roadrunner that was roosting, nesting, or feeding in their yard. With what affection they spoke about the bird! Most gave a name to their wild "pet" and put out food for it. Many reported that after the bird had been around for a while, it would take food from their hands. I don't doubt this, as I have had the pleasure of feeding a wild roadrunner by hand too. Truly, the roadrunner is a bird of the people.

Bibliography

Abbott, C. G. 1940. Household road-runners. *Condor* 42:119–21.

Allen, P. E. 1950. Road-runner in eastern Oklahoma. *Condor* 52:43.

Allen, W. E. 1932. Notes of food of California roadrunner (*Geococcyx californianus*). *Bird-Lore* 34:264–5.

American Ornithologists' Union. 1886. *The code of nomenclature and check-list of North American birds.* New York: Am. Ornithol. Union.

———. 1910. *Check-list of North American birds.* 3rd ed. rev. New York: Am. Ornithol. Union.

———. 1931. *Check-list of North American birds.* 4th ed. Lancaster, Pa.: Am. Ornithol. Union.

———. 1957. *Check-list of North American birds.* 5th ed. Ithaca, N.Y.: Am. Ornithol. Union.

———. 1983. *Check-list of North American birds.* 6th ed. Washington, D.C.: Am. Ornithol. Union.

Amon, A. 1978. *Roadrunners and other cuckoos.* New York: Atheneum.

Andrews, R., and R. Righter. 1992. *Colorado birds: a reference to their distribution and habitat.* Denver: Denver Mus. of Nat. Hist.

Anthony, A. W. 1892. Birds of southwestern New Mexico. *Auk* 9:357–69.

———. 1896. The roadrunner as a rat-killer. *Auk* 13:257–58.

———. 1897. The roadrunner as a destroyer of caterpillars. *Auk* 14:217.

Arizona Game and Fish Department. N.d. Arizona Breeding Bird Atlas. Unpublished data (1993–2001), Ariz. Game and Fish Dept., Nongame Branch. Phoenix.

Arkansas Natural Heritage Commission. 2002. Arkansas' rare species. http://naturalheritage.com/publications/rare/ (accessed February 4, 2004).

Austin, G. T. 1970. Breeding birds of desert riparian habitat in southern Nevada. *Condor* 72:431–36.

Baerg, W. J. 1950. Occurrence of the roadrunner in Arkansas. *Condor* 52:165.

———. 1951. *Birds of Arkansas.* Fayetteville: Univ. of Ariz. Coll. of Agric.

Bailey, A. M., and R. J. Niedrach. 1965. *Birds of Colorado.* Denver: Denver Mus. of Nat. Hist.

Bailey, F. M. 1917. *Handbook of birds of the western United States.* Boston: Houghton Mifflin.

———. 1922. Koo. *Bird-Lore* 24:260–65.

———. 1923. Birds recorded from the Santa Rita Mountains in southern Arizona. *Pac. Coast Avifauna*, no. 15.

———. 1928. *Birds of New Mexico*. New Mex. Dept. of Game and Fish in cooperation with the State Game Protective Assoc. and the Bur. of Biol. Surv. Washington, D.C.: Judd and Detweiler Press.

Baird, S. F. 1859. Birds of the boundary. In *United States and Mexican Boundary Survey under the Order of Lieut. Col. W. H. Emory*. Washington, D.C.

Bancroft, G. 1930. The breeding birds of central lower California. *Condor* 32:20–49.

Barclay, J. S. 1977. Roadrunner takes birds from mist net. *Bird-Banding* 48:280.

Bartholomew, G. A., T. R. Howell, and T. J. Cade. 1957. Torpidity in the white-throated swift, Anna hummingbird, and poor-will. *Condor* 59:145–55.

Baumgartner, F. M., and A. M. Baumgartner. 1992. *Oklahoma bird life*. Norman: Univ. Okla. Press.

Beal, K. G. 1978. Year-round weather-dependent behavior of the roadrunner (*Geococcyx californianus*). PhD diss., Ohio State Univ., Columbus.

———. 1981. Winter foraging habits of the roadrunner. *Bull. Okla. Ornithol. Soc.* 14:13–15.

Beal, K. G., and R. E. Beal. 1978. Immature Cooper's hawk attempts to capture roadrunner. *Bull. Okla. Ornithol. Soc.* 11:31.

Beal, K. G., and L. D. Gillam. 1979. On the function of prey beating by roadrunners. *Condor* 81:85–87.

Behle, W. H. 1943. Birds of Pine Valley Mountain region, southwestern Utah. *Bull. Univ. Utah* 34:1–85.

———. 1944. Checklist of the birds of Utah. *Condor* 46:67–87.

———. 1960. *The birds of southeastern Utah*. Univ. Utah Biol. Ser., vol. 12, no. 1. Salt Lake City: Univ. of Utah.

———. 1963. Avifaunistic analysis of the Great Basin region of North America. *Proc. 13th Int. Ornithol. Congr.*: 1168–1181.

Bendire, C. E. 1878. Breeding habits of *Geococcyx californianus*. *Bull. Nuttall Ornithol. Club* 3:39.

———. 1895. Life histories of North American birds. *U.S. Nat. Mus. Spec. Bull. 3*. Wash., D.C.: Gov. Printing Office.

Benedict, R. 1935. *Zuni mythology*. Columbia Univ. Contrib. Anthropol., vol. 2, no. 1. New York: Colombia Univ. Press.

———. 1948. *Tales of the Cochiti Indians*. Albuquerque: Univ. New Mex. Press.

Berger, A. J. 1952. The comparative functional morphology of the pelvic appendage in three genera of Cuculidae. *Am. Midl. Nat.* 47:513–605.

———. 1954. The myology of the pectoral appendages of three genera of American cuckoos. *Misc. Publ. Mus. Zool Univ. Mich.* 85:5–35.

———. 1960. Some anatomical characteristics of the Cuculidae and Muscophagidae. *Wilson Bull.* 72:60–104.

Binford, L. C. 1971. Roadrunner captures orchard oriole in California. *Calif. Birds* 2:139.

Birkenstein, L. R., and R. E. Tomlinson. 1981. *Native names of Mexican birds*. Washington D.C.: U.S. Dept. of Interior, Fish and Wildl. Serv. Resour. Publ. 139.

Blake, E. R. 1953. *Birds of Mexico*. Chicago: Univ. Chicago Press.

Bleich, V. C. 1975. Roadrunner predation on ground squirrels in California. *Auk* 92:147–49.

Brecheisen, W. R. 1956. Roadrunner in eastern Kansas. *Kans. Ornithol. Soc. Bull.* 7:5.

Brown, L. N. 1963. Status of the roadrunner in Missouri. *Condor* 65:242–43.

Bryant, H. C. 1916. Habits and food of the roadrunner in California. *Univ. Calif. Publ. Zool.* 17:21–58.

Calder, W. A. 1966. Temperature regulation and respiration in the roadrunner and the pigeon. PhD diss., Duke Univ., Durham, N.C.

———. 1967a. Breeding behavior of the roadrunner, *Geococcyx californianus*. *Auk* 84:597–98.

———. 1967b. The diurnal activity of the roadrunner, *Geococcyx californianus*. *Condor* 70:84–85.

———. 1968. Nest sanitation: a possible factor in the water economy of the roadrunner. *Condor* 70:279.

———. 1984. *Size, function, and life history*. Cambridge, Mass.: Harvard Univ. Press.

Calder, W. A., and P. J. Bentley. 1967. Urine concentrations of two carnivorous birds, the white pelican and the roadrunner. *Comp. Biochem. Physiol.* 22:607–609.

Calder, W. A., and K. Schmidt-Nielsen. 1967. Temperature regulation and evaporation in the pigeon and the roadrunner. *Am. J. Physiol.* 213:883–89.

Carpenter, M. C., and J. I. Mead. 2003. Late Pleistocene roadrunner (*Geococcyx*) from Kartchner Caverns State Park, southeastern Arizona. *Southwest. Nat.* 48:402–10.

Colton, H. S. 1959. *Hopi kachina dolls*. Albuquerque: Univ. New Mex. Press.

Colvin, W. 1935. Roadrunner nesting in Kansas. *Auk* 52:88.

Cornell Laboratory of Ornithology, Bird Population Studies. N.d. North American nest record card program data for the roadrunner. Cornell Univ., Ithaca, N.Y.

Cornett, J. W. 1983. Early nesting of the roadrunner, *Geococcyx californianus*, in California. *Am. Birds* 37:236.

———. 1998. Does the greater roadrunner hibernate? *San Bernardino Co. Mus. Q.* 45:103.

———. 1999. Roadrunner attack on juvenile desert tortoise. *San Bernardino Co. Mus. Q.* 46:57–58.

———. 2000. Unusual foraging strategy by the greater roadrunner. *West. Birds* 31:61–62.

———. 2001. *The roadrunner*. Palm Springs, Calif.: Nature Trails Press.

Cottam, D., C. S. Williams, and C. A. Sooter. 1942. Flight and running speeds of birds. *Wilson Bull.* 54:121–31.

Coues, E. 1874. *Birds of the Northwest: a handbook of the ornithology of the region drained by the Missouri River and its tributaries*. U.S. Geol. Geogr. Surv. Territ., Misc. Publ. no. 3. Washington, D.C.: Gov. Printing Office.

———. 1900. The "Churca"(*Geococcyx californianus*). *Auk* 17:70.

Curtin, L. S. M. 1949. *By the prophet of the earth: ethnobotany of the Pima*. Repr., Tucson: Univ. Ariz. Press, 1984.

Cutright, P. R., and M. J. Brodhead. 1972. *Elliott Coues: naturalist and frontier historian*. Urbana: Univ. Ill. Press.

Davis, W. B., and D. J. Schmidly. 1997. The mammals of Texas—online edition: nine-banded armadillo. http://www.nsrl.ttu.edu/tmot1/dasynove.htm (accessed February 5, 2004).

Dawson, W. L. 1923. *Birds of California*. Vol. 3. San Diego: South Moulton Co.

Dawson, W. R., and G. A. Bartholomew. 1968. Temperature regulation and water economy of desert birds. In *Desert biology*, vol. 1, ed. G. W. Brown, pp. 357–94. New York: Academic Press.

Dawson, W. R., and K. Schmidt-Nielsen. 1964. Terrestrial animals in dry heat: desert birds. In *Handbook of physiology*, sec. 4, *Adaptations to the environment*, ed. D. B. Dill, pp. 481–92. Washington, D.C.: Am. Physiol. Soc.

DiPeso, C., J. B. Rinaldo, and G. J. Fenner. 1974. *Casas Grandes: a fallen trading center of the Gran Chichimeca*. Amerind Foundation Publications, vol. 6, no. 9. Flagstaff, Ariz.: Northland Press.

Dixon, K. L. 1959. Ecological and distributional relations of desert scrub birds of western Texas. *Condor* 61:397–409.

Dobie, J. F. 1939. The roadrunner in fact and folk-lore. Repr. for the Tex. Game, Fish, and Oyster Comm. from *In the shadow of history*, ed. J. F. Dobie, M. C. Boatright, and H. H. Ransom, pp. 1–31. Austin: Tex. Folk-Lore Soc.

———. 1978. The paisano's cactus corral. In *Paisanos: a folklore miscellany*, ed. F. E. Abernethy, pp. 3–9. Austin, Tex.: Encino Press.

Douglas, V. 1984. *Roadrunner*. Happy Camp, Calif.: Naturegraph Publ.

Dresser, H. E. 1865. Notes of the birds of southern Texas. *Ibis*, n.s., 1:466–67.

Dumarest, N., Father. 1919. Notes on Cochiti, New Mexico. *Am. Anthropol. Assoc.* Mem. 6:137–236.

Dunning, J. S. 1987. *South American birds*. Newtown Square, Pa.: Harrowood Books.

Dunson, W. A., M. K. Dunson, and R. D. Ohmart. 1976. Evidence for the presence of nasal salt glands in the roadrunner and the *Coturnix* quail. *J. Exp. Zool.* 198:209–16.

Eltaher, H. 1980. Acceptance and rejection of parasitic eggs by the road-runner female *Geococcyx californianus* and the Gambel's quail female *Lophortyx gambeli*. *J. Coll. Sci. Univ. Riyadh* 11:85–94.

Emlen, J. T. 1974. An urban bird community in Tucson, Arizona: derivation, structure, regulation. *Condor* 76:184–97.

Engels, W. L. 1938. Cursorial adaptations in birds: limb proportions in the skeleton of *Geococcyx*. *J. Morphol.* 63:207–17.

Fewkes, J. W. 1903. *Hopi katcinas drawn by native artists*. Smithson. Inst. Bur. Am. Ethnol. Annu. Rep. Repr., Glorieta, N.Mex.: Rio Grande Press.

Finch, D. M. 1981. Nest predation of Abert's towhees by coachwhips and roadrunners. *Condor* 83:389.

Finley, W. L., and I. Finley. 1915. With the Arizona roadrunners. *Bird Lore* 17:159–65.

Fisher, A. K. 1893. *Report on birds—the Death Valley expedition*. U.S. Dept. Agric., Div. Ornithol. Mammal. Washington, D.C.: Gov. Printing Office.

Fisher, W. K. 1904. Road-runners eat young mockingbirds. *Condor* 6:80.

Folse, L. J., Jr. 1974. Population ecology of roadrunners (*Geococcyx californianus*) in South Texas. MS thesis, Tex. A&M Univ., College Station.

Folse, L. J., Jr., and K. A. Arnold. 1976. Secondary sex characteristics in roadrunners. *Bird-Banding* 47:115–18.

———. 1978. Population ecology of roadrunners (*Geococcyx californianus*) in South Texas. *Southwest. Nat.* 23:1–28.

Ford, R. I., ed. 1986. *An ethnobiology source book: the uses of plants and animals by American Indians*. New York: Garland.

Friedman, H. 1933. A contribution to the life-history of the crespin or four-winged cuckoo, *Tapera naevia*. *Ibis* 75:532–39.

Friedman, H., L. Griscom, and R. T. Moore. 1950. Distributional check-list of the birds of Mexico. *Pac. Coast Avifauna* 29:136–37.

Gander, F. F. 1958. The roadrunner. *Audubon Mag.* (January–February): 24–26.

Gehlbach, F. R., and J. A. Holman. 1974. Paleoecology of amphibians and reptiles from Pratt Cave, Guadalupe Mountains National Park, Texas. *Southwest. Nat.* 19:191–98.

Geluso, K. N. 1969. Food and survival problems of Oklahoma roadrunners in winter. *Bull. Okla. Ornithol. Soc.* 2:5–6.

———. 1970a. Additional notes on food and fat of roadrunners in winter. *Bull. Okla. Ornithol. Soc.* 3:6.

———. 1970b. Feeding behavior of a roadrunner in winter. *Bull. Okla. Ornithol. Soc.* 3:32.

Goertz, J. W., and E. E. Mowbray. 1971. Nesting records for three species of Louisiana birds. *Southwest. Nat.* 15:265–66.

Gorsuch, D. M. 1932. The roadrunner. *Ariz. Wild Life* (October): 1–11.

Goss, N. S. 1886. *A revised catalogue of the birds of Kansas*. Topeka: Kans. Publ. House.

Green, C. A. 1994. Roadrunner predation on purple martins. *Purple Martin Update* 5:12.

Green, J. W. 1967. Rock art of the El Paso Southwest: Fusselman Canyon petroglyph site EPAS–44. *The Artifact* 5 (1):1–19.

Greene, E., D. Wilcove, and M. McFarland. 1984. Observations of birds at an army ant swarm in Guerrero, Mexico. *Condor* 86:92–93.

Grinnell, J. 1893. Nesting of the roadrunner. *Science* 21:247.

———. 1907. The California distribution of the roadrunner (*Geococcyx californianus*). *Condor* 9:51–53.

———. 1911. A distributional list of the birds of California. *Pac. Coast Avifauna*, no. 11.

———. 1914. *An account of the mammals and birds of the lower Colorado Valley*. Univ. Calif. Publ. Biol., no. 12. Repr., New York: Arno Press, 1978.

Grinnell, J., and A. H. Miller. 1944. The distribution of the birds of California. *Pac. Coast Avifauna*, no. 27.

Haffer, J. 1977. A systematic review of the neotropical ground cuckoos Aves—*Neomorphus*. *Bonn. Zool. Beitr.* 28(1–2): 48–76.

Hamilton, T. H. 1962. The habitats of the avifauna of the mesquite plains of Texas. *Am. Midl. Nat.* 67:85–105.

Hamilton, W. J., and M. E. Hamilton. 1965. Breeding characteristics of yellow-billed cuckoos in Arizona. *Proc. Calif. Acad. Sci.* 32:405–32.

Harris, A. H., and C. R. Crews. 1983. Conkling's roadrunner—a subspecies of the California roadrunner? *Southwest. Nat.* 28:407–12.

Harrison, C. J. O. 1971. The sunbathing of the roadrunner. *Aviculture Mag.* 77:128.

Hayward, C. L., C. Cottam, A. M. Woodbury, and H. H. Frost. 1976. *Birds of Utah*. Great Basin Nat. Mem., no. 1.

Herreid, C. F., II. 1960. Roadrunner a predator of bats. *Condor* 62:67.

Herrick, F. H. 1910. Life and behavior of the cuckoo. *J. Exp. Zool.* 9:169–233.

Hibben, F. C. 1975. *Kiva art of the Anasazi at Pottery Mound*. Las Vegas, Nev.: KC Publ.

Hilton-Taylor, C., comp. 2000. *2000 IUCN red list of threatened species*. Gland, Switzerland, and Cambridge, UK: Int. Union for the Conserv. of Nat.

Holland, H. M. 1917. The valley quail occupying nest of the roadrunner. *Condor* 19:23–24.

Holt, H. R., and J. A. Lane. 1987. *A birder's guide to Colorado*. Denver: L and P Press.

Holte, A. E., and M. A. Houck. 2000. Juvenile greater roadrunner (Cuculidae) killed by choking on a Texas horned lizard (*Phrynosoma*). *Southwest. Nat.* 45:74–76.

Holterhoff, E., Jr. 1881. A collector's notes on the breeding of a few western birds. *Am. Nat.* 5:208–19.

Holterhoff, G., Jr. 1883. *Geococcyx* as a vocalist. *Bull. Nuttall Ornithol. Club* 8:182–83.

Howard, H. 1931. A new species of road-runner from Quaternary cave deposits in New Mexico. *Condor* 33:206–209.

———. 1962. A comparison of avian assemblages from individual pits at Rancho La Brea, California. *Los Ang. Cty. Mus. Contrib. Sci.* 58:1–24.

Howell, A. B. 1916. Some results of a winter's observations in Arizona. *Condor* 18:209–14.

Howell, S. N. G., and S. Webb. 1995. *A guide to the birds of Mexico and northern central America*. New York: Oxford Univ. Press.

Hughes, J. M. 1996a. *Greater roadrunner (Geococcyx californianus)*. The birds of North America, no. 244, ed. A. Poole and F. Gill. Philadelphia: Acad. Nat. Sci.; Washington, D.C.: Am. Ornithol. Union.

———. 1996b. Phylogenetic analysis of the Cuculidae (Aves, Cuculiformes) using behavioral and ecological characters. *Auk* 113:10–22.

Hughes, M. R. 1970. Relative kidney size in nonpasserine birds with functional salt glands. *Condor* 72:164–68.

Hunt, R. 1920. How fast can a roadrunner run? *Condor* 22:186–87.

Igl, L. D. 1996. Bird checklists of the United States. Jamestown, N.D.: Northern Prairie Wildlife Research Center Home Page. http://www.npwrc.usgs.gov/resource/othrdata/chekbird/chekbird.htm (version. 12MAY03) (accessed January 26, 2004).

Ingersoll, E. 1923. *Birds in legend, fable, and folklore*. New York: Longmans, Green, and Co.

Jaeger, E. C. 1947. Stone-turning habits of some desert birds. *Condor* 49:171.

———. 1948. Does the poor-will hibernate? *Condor* 50:45–46.

———. 1949. Further observations of the hibernation of the poor-will. *Condor* 5:105–109.

James, D. A., and J. C. Neal. 1986. *Arkansas birds: their distribution and abundance*. Fayetteville: Univ. Arkansas Press.

Jensen, J. K. 1923. Notes on the nesting birds of northern Santa Fe County, New Mexico. *Auk* 40:452–69.

Johnsgard, P. A. 1980. *Birds of the Great Plains: breeding species and their distribution*. Lincoln: Univ. Nebr. Press.

Johnson, D. H., M. D. Bryant, and A. H. Miller. 1948. *Vertebrate animals of the Providence Mountains area of California*. Berkeley and Los Angeles: Univ. Calif. Press.

Jones, C. 1999. *Chuck Amuck*. Ottawa, Ontario: Farrar, Straus, and Giroux.

Kaeding, G. L. 1906. New bird for Amador County. *Condor* 8:57.

Kansas Bird Records Committee. 2002. 1990–2001 report of the Kansas Bird Records Committee. http://www.ksbirds.org/KBRC/kbrc_summary1990-2001.htm (accessed February 3, 2004).

Kavanau, J. L., and J. Ramos. 1970. Roadrunners: activity of captive individuals. *Science* 169:780–82.

Kazmaier, R. T., D. C. Ruthven III, and D. R. Synatzske. 1999. Spring and summer diets of greater roadrunners in South Texas. In *Wildlife Research Highlights*, vol. 4, ed. Ray C. Telfair II. Austin: Tex. Parks Wildl. Dept.

Kellogg, V. L. 1893. The road-runner in Kansas. *Auk* 10:364–65.

Kelsey, F. W. 1903. The home of the California roadrunner. *Condor* 5:132–33.

Kilgore, D. L., M. H. Bernstein, and D. M. Hudson. 1976. Brain temperatures in birds. *J. Comp. Physiol.* 110:209–15.

Kimsey, J. B. 1958. Northward extension of the range of the California roadrunner in California. *Condor* 55:215–16.

Koes, R. F. 1991. Additions to the Manitoba bird list (1985–1990). *Blue Jay* 49:4.

Lacey, H. 1911. The birds of Kerrville, Texas, and vicinity. *Auk* 28:200–219.

Lack, D. 1940. Courtship feeding in birds. *Auk* 57:169–78.

Ladd, E. J. 1963. Zuni ethno-ornithology. MS thesis, Univ. New Mex., Albuquerque.

Lange, C. H. 1959. *Cochiti, a New Mexico pueblo, past and present*. Carbondale: South. Ill. Univ. Press.

Larson, L. M. 1930. Osteology of the California road-runner recent and Pleistocene. *Univ. Calif. Publ. Zool.* 32:409–28.

Lasiewski, R. C., M. H. Bernstein, and R. D. Ohmart. 1971. Cutaneous water loss in the roadrunner and poorwill. *Condor* 73:470–72.

Law, J. E. 1923. A guilty road-runner: circumstantial evidence. *Condor* 25:33–34.

Leopold, A. 1922. Road-runner caught in the act. *Condor* 24:183.

Lewis, A. H. 1897. The road runner corrals a rattlesnake. In *A treasury of western folklore*, ed. B. A. Botkin, pp. 295–301. Repr., New York: Bonanza Books, 1980.

Ligon, J. S. 1961. *New Mexico birds and where to find them*. Albuquerque: Univ. New Mex. Press.

Linsdale, J. M. 1936. The birds of Nevada. *Pac. Coast Avifauna*, no. 23.

Longacre, W. A., S. J. Holbrook, and M. W. Graves. 1982. Multidisciplinary research at Grasshopper Pueblo, Arizona. *Anthropol. Pap. Univ. Ariz.*, no. 40. Tucson: Univ. Ariz. Press.

Louisiana Department of Wildlife and Fisheries. N.d. Louisiana Natural Heritage Program. http://www.wlf. state.la.us/apps/netgear/index.asp?cn=lawlf&pid=569 (accessed February 5, 2004).

Lowe, C. H., and D. S. Hinds. 1969. Thermoregulation in desert populations of roadrunners and doves. In *Physiological systems in semiarid environments*, ed. C. C. Hoff and M. L. Riedesel, p. 113. Albuquerque: Univ. New Mex. Press.

Lowery, G. H. J. 1974. *Louisiana birds*. 3rd ed. Baton Rouge: La. State Univ. Press.

Machula, O. R. N.d. Dlö Binantá—an original Apache tale. http://www.geocities.com/~zybt/dlo.htm.

McAtee, W. L. 1931. A little essay on vermin. *Bird-Lore* 33:379–84.

Mailliard, J. 1900. Land birds of Marin County, California. *Condor* 2:62–68.

Marshall, J. T., Jr. 1957. Birds of pine-oak woodland in southern Arizona and adjacent Mexico. *Pac. Coast Avifauna*, no. 32. Berkeley, Calif.: Cooper Ornithol. Soc.

——— 1963. Fire and bird in the mountains of southern Arizona. In *Proceedings Second Annual Tall Timber Fire Ecology Conference*. Tallahassee, Fla.: Tall Timbers Res. Stn.

Marshall, M. E. 1907. Studies of avian anatomy. II. *Geococcyx, Bubo,* and *Aeronautes. Trans. Tex. Acad. Sci.* 9:19–41.

Martin, A. C., H. S. Zim, and A. L. Nelson. 1951. *American wildlife and plants*. New York: Dover Publ.

Martin, L. D., and R. M. Mengel. 1984. A new cuckoo and a chachalaca from the early Miocene of Colorado. *Spec. Publ. Carnegie Mus. Nat. Hist.* 9:171–77.

Meinzer, W. 1993. *The roadrunner*. Lubbock: Tex. Tech Univ. Press.

Michael, E. D. 1967. Behavioral interactions of birds and white-tailed deer. *Condor* 69:431–32.

Miller, A. H. 1932. Observations on some breeding birds of El Salvador, Central America. *Condor* 34:13–14.

Miller, F. 1879. Strange story of a California bird. *Bull. Nuttall Ornithol. Club* 4:109–10.

Miller, L. 1943. The Pleistocene birds of San Josecito Cavern, Mexico. *Univ. Calif. Publ. Zool.* 47:143–68.

Missouri Department of Conservation. 2003. Natural Heritage Database; Missouri species of conservation concern checklist. http://mdc.mo.gov/nathis/endangered/checklst/ (accessed February 5, 2004).

Montoya, A. B., P. J. Zwank, and M. Cardenas. 1997. Breeding biology of aplomado falcons in desert grassland of Chihuahua, Mexico. *J. Field Ornithol.* 68:135–43.

Muller, K. A. 1971. Physical and behavioral development of a roadrunner raised at the National Zoological Park. *Wilson Bull.* 83:186–93.

Napier, A. 1969. The clown that met the wagon trains. *Front. Times* 43(2): 34–35, 52–54.

Neeld, F., and S. E. English. 1992. Late nesting of greater roadrunner in Carter County, Oklahoma. *Bull. Okla. Ornithol. Soc.* 25:21.

Newberry, J. S. 1857. *Reports on the geology, botany, and zoology of Northern California and Oregon, made to the War Department*. Vol. 6 of *Pacific Railroad survey*. Washington, D.C.: Gov. Printing Office.

Nice, M. M. 1931. *The birds of Oklahoma*. Norman: Univ. Okla. Press.

Norris, D. J., and W. H. Elder. 1982. Decline of the roadrunner in Missouri. *Wilson Bull*. 94:354–55.

Oberholser, H. C. 1925. The relations of vegetation to bird life in Texas. *Am. Midl. Nat*. 9:564–66l.

———. 1974. *The Bird Life of Texas*. Vol. 1. Austin: Univ. Tex. Press.

Ohmart, R. D. 1972. Physiological and ecological observations concerning the salt secreting nasal glands of the roadrunner. *Comp. Biochem. Physiol*. 43a: 311–16.

———. 1973. Observations on the breeding adaptations of the roadrunner. *Condor* 75:140–49.

———. 1989. A timid desert creature that appears to be half bird, half reptile. *Nat. Hist*. 89:34–40.

Ohmart, R. D., and R. C. Lasiewski. 1971. Roadrunners: energy conservation by hypothermia and absorption of sunlight. *Science* 172:67–69.

Ohmart, R. D., T. E. Chapman, and L. Z. McFarland. 1970. Water turnover in roadrunners under different environmental conditions. *Auk* 87:787–93.

Ohmart, R. D., L. Z. McFarland, and J. P. Morgan. 1970. Urographic evidence that urine enters the rectum and ceca of the roadrunner *Geococcyx californianus* Aves. *Comp. Biochem. Physiol*. 35:487–89.

Orcutt, C. R. 1886. Roadrunners corralling rattlesnakes. *West. Am. Scientist* 2:49.

Oregon Bird Records Committee. 2003. Unaccepted records of the Oregon Bird Records Committee. http://www.oregonbirds.org/unaccepted_recs.html (accessed February 7, 2004).

Parmley, D. 1982. Food items of roadrunners from Palo Pinto County, north central Texas. *Tex. J. Sci*. 34:94–95.

Parsons, E. C. 1924. *The scalp ceremony of Zuni*. Mem. Am. Anthropol. Assoc., no. 31. Menasha, Wisc.

———. 1929. *The social organization of the Tewa of New Mexico*. Mem. Am. Anthropol. Assoc., no. 36. Menasha, Wisc.

———. 1939. *Pueblo Indian religion*. Vols. 1 and 2. Chicago: Univ. Chicago Press.

Patuxent Wildlife Research Center. N.d. Food habits card file for greater roadrunner. U.S. Geol. Surv., Patuxent Wildl. Res. Cent., Laurel, Md.

Patuxent Wildlife Research Center Bird Banding Laboratory. N.d. Unpublished banding and recapture records for greater roadrunner. U.S. Geol. Surv., Patuxent Wildl. Res. Cent., Laurel, Md.

Pemberton, J. R. 1916. Variation of the broken-wing stunt by a roadrunner. *Condor* 18:203.

———. 1925. Parasitism in the roadrunner. *Condor* 27:35.

Perrins, C. M. 1970. The timing of birds breeding seasons. *Ibis* 112:242–55.

Peters, J. L. 1940. *Checklist of birds of the world*. Vol. 4. Cambridge, Mass.: Harvard Univ. Press.

Petersen, P. C. 1970. Middle western prairie region. *Audubon Field Notes* 24:608–15.

Phelps, W. H., and R. M. de Schauensee. 1978. *A guide to the birds of Venezuela*. Princeton, N.J.: Princeton Univ. Press.

Phillips, A., J. Marshall, and G. Monson. 1964. *The birds of Arizona*. Tucson: Univ. Ariz. Press.

Price, J., S. Droege, and A. Price. 1995. *The summer atlas of North American breeding birds*. London: Academic Press.

Probasco, G. E. 1976. Bird habitat—woody plant relations on Missouri limestone glades. In *Proceedings of the Fifth Midwest Prairie Conference*, ed. D. Glenn-Lewis and R. Q. Landers, pp. 107–109. Ames: Iowa State Univ. Press.

Prophet, C. W. 1957. Nesting record of the roadrunner in Kansas. *Kans. Ornithol. Soc. Bull*. 8:10.

Pulich, W. M. 1988. *The birds of north central Texas*. College Station: Tex. A&M Univ. Press.

Pyle, P. 1997. *Identification guide to North American birds*. Bolinas, Calif.: Slate Creek Press.

Rand, A. L. 1941. Courtship of the roadrunner. *Auk* 58:57–59.

Rappole, J. H. 1994. *Birds of Texas: a field guide*. College Station: Tex. A&M Univ. Press.

Rappole, J. H., and G. W. Blacklock. 1985. *Birds of the Texas Coastal Bend: abundance and distribution*. College Station: Tex. A&M Univ. Press.

Rea, A. M. 1981. Resource utilization and food taboos of Sonoran Desert peoples. *J. Ethnobiol.* 1:69–83.

Ridgway, R. 1916. *The birds of North and Middle America.* Bull. U.S. Natl. Mus., no. 50, pt. 7. Washington, D.C.: Gov. Printing Office.

Robbins, M. B., and D. A. Easterla. 1992. *Birds of Missouri.* Columbia: Univ. Mo. Press.

Root, T. 1988. *Atlas of wintering North American birds: an analysis of Christmas Bird Count data.* Chicago: Univ. Chicago Press.

Roth, P. 1981. A nest of the rufous-vented ground-cuckoo *Neomorphus geoffroyi. Condor* 83:388.

Roth, R. R. 1971. Ecological features of bird communities in South Texas brush-grasslands. PhD diss., Univ. Ill., Urbana.

———. 1977. The composition of four bird communities in South Texas brush grasslands. *Condor* 79:417–25.

Rylander, M. K. 1972. Winter dormitory of the roadrunner, *Geococcyx californianus*, in West Texas. *Auk* 89:896.

Ryser, F. A., Jr. 1985. *Birds of the Great Basin—a natural history.* Reno: Univ. Nev. Press.

Sauer, J. R., J. E. Hines, and J. Fallon. 2003. *The North American breeding bird survey, results and analysis 1966–2002.* Version 2003.1. U.S. Geol. Surv., Patuxent Wildl. Res. Cent., Laurel, Md.

Schaafsma, P. 1980. *Indian rock art of the Southwest.* Albuquerque: Univ. New Mex. Press.

———. 1989. Supper or symbol: roadrunner tracks in Southwest art and ritual. In *Animals into art*, ed. H. Morphy, pp. 253–69. London: Unwin Hyman.

Schmidly, D. J. 2002. *Texas natural history: a century of change.* Lubbock: Tex. Tech Univ. Press.

Sealy, S. B. 1985. Erect posture of the young black-billed cuckoo: an adaptation for early mobility in a nomadic species. *Auk* 102:889–92.

Selander, R. K., and D. K. Hunter. 1960. On the functions of wing-flashing in mockingbirds. *Wilson Bull.* 72:341–48.

Sheldon, H. H. 1922. Top speed of the roadrunner. *Condor* 24:180.

Shepardson, D. I. 1915. Some western birds—roadrunner. *Oologist* 32:158–60.

Sherbrooke, W. C. 1990. Predatory behavior of captive greater roadrunners feeding on horned lizards. *Wilson Bull.* 102:171–74.

Shetlar, D. J. 1971. Winter food of a central Oklahoma roadrunner. *Bull. Okla. Ornithol. Soc.* 4:35.

Shufeldt, R. W. 1885. On the coloration in life of the naked skin-tracts on the head of *Geococcyx californianus. Ibis*, 5th ser., 3:286–88.

———. 1886a. Contributions to the anatomy of *Geococcyx californianus. Proc. Zool. Soc. London* 1886:466–90.

———. 1886b. The skeleton in *Geococcyx. J. Anat. Physiol.* 20:244–66.

———. 1903. The chaparral cock. *Pac. Coast Mag./West. Field* 2:174–79.

Siegel, C. E., J. M. Hamilton, and N. R. Castro. 1989. Observations of the red-billed ground-cuckoo *Neomorphus pucheranii* in association with tamarins (*Saguinus*) in northeastern Amazonian Peru. *Condor* 91:720–22.

Sieving, K. R. 1990. Pheasant cuckoo foraging behavior, with notes on habits and possible social organization in Panama. *J. Field Ornithol.* 61:41–46.

Simmons, G. F. 1925. *Birds of the Austin region.* Austin: Univ. Tex. Press.

Skutch, A. F. 1966. Life history notes on three tropical American cuckoos. *Wilson Bull.* 78:139–65.

———. 1976. *Parent birds and their young.* Austin: Univ. Tex. Press.

———. 1983. *Birds of tropical America.* Austin: Univ. Tex. Press.

Sloanaker, J. L. 1913. Bird notes from the South-west. *Wilson Bull.* 25:187–99.

Small, A. 1994. *California birds: their status and distribution.* Vista, Calif.: Ibis.

Smith, M. H. 1980. Breeding the roadrunner, *Geococcyx californiana*, at Columbia Zoo. *Int. Zoo Yearb.* 21:119–21.

Smithers, W. D. N.d. Nature's pharmacy and the curanderos. In *Pancho Villa's last hangout—on both sides of the Rio Grande in the Big Bend country.* N.p.

Smyth, M., and H. N. Coulombe. 1971. Notes on the use of desert springs by birds in California. *Condor* 73:240–43.

Snow, F. H. 1904. The black-bellied plover, road-runner, and black-throated green warbler in Kansas. *Auk* 21:85–86.

Spencer, O. R. 1943. Nesting habits of the black-billed cuckoo. *Wilson Bull.* 55:11–22.

Spofford, S. H. 1976. Roadrunner catches hummingbird in flight. *Condor* 78:142.

———. 1978. Roadrunners as predators on birds in banding traps. *North Am. Bird Bander* 3:55.

Steadman, D. W., J. Arroyo-Cabrales, E. Johnson, and A. F. Guzman. 1994. New information on the late Pleistocene birds from San Josecito Cave, Nuevo Leòn, Mexico. *Condor* 96:577–89.

Stevenson, M. C. 1904. The Zuñi Indians: their mythology, esoteric fraternities, and ceremonies. In *Twenty-third Annual Report of the Bureau of American Ethnology, 1901–1902, to the Secretary of the Smithsonian Institution*, ed. J. W. Powell, pp. 1–684. Washington, D.C.: Gov. Printing Office.

Stiles, F. G., A. F. Skutch, and D. Gardner. 1989. *A guide to the birds of Costa Rica*. Ithaca, N.Y.: Cornell Univ. Press.

Stimson, F. B. 1975. Persecuted roadrunner. *Def. Wildl.* 50:340–41.

Sutton, G. M. 1913. A pet roadrunner. *Bird-Lore* 15:324.

———. 1915. Suggestive methods of bird study: pet roadrunners. *Bird-Lore* 17:57–61.

———. 1922. Notes on the road-runner at Ft. Worth, Texas. *Wilson Bull.* 34:2–20.

———. 1936. *Birds in the wilderness*. New York: Macmillan.

———. 1940. *Geococcyx californianus* (Lesson), roadrunner. In *Life histories of North American cuckoos, goatsuckers, hummingbirds, and their allies*, pt. 1, ed. A. C. Bent, pp. 36–51. U.S. Natl. Mus. Bull., no. 176. Repr., New York: Dover Publ., 1964.

———. 1967. *Oklahoma birds: their ecology and distribution, with comments on the avifauna of the southern Great Plains*. Norman: Univ. Okla. Press.

———. 1973. Winter food of a central Oklahoma roadrunner. *Bull. Okla. Ornithol. Soc.* 5:30.

———. 1977. *Fifty common birds of Oklahoma and the southern Great Plains*. Norman: Univ. Okla. Press.

———. 1986. *Birds worth watching*. Norman: Univ. Okla. Press.

Taber, W. 1951. Roadrunner in Oklahoma. *Condor* 53:101.

Terres, J. K. 1987. *Audubon encyclopedia of North American birds*. New York: Alfred A. Knopf.

Thompson, M. C., and C. Ely. 1989. *Birds in Kansas*. Vol. 1. Lawrence: Univ. Kans. Mus. Nat. Hist.

Tomoff, C. S. 1972. Breeding bird diversities in the Sonoran Desert creosotebush association. PhD diss., Univ. Ariz., Tucson.

Trimble, S. 1993. *The people: Indians of the American Southwest*. Santa Fe, New Mex.: SAR Press.

Trowbridge, A. H., and H. L. Whitaker. 1934. Some observations on birds in southeastern Oklahoma. *Wilson Bull.* 46:240–42.

Tyler, H. A. 1979. *Pueblo birds and myths*. Norman: Univ. Okla. Press.

Van Devender, T. R. 1977. Holocene woodlands in the Southwestern deserts. *Science* 198:189–92.

Van Dyke, T. S. N.d. The roadrunner and the snake. *Avifauna* 1:36–38.

Van Tyne, J., and G. M. Sutton. 1937. The birds of Brewster County, Texas. *Misc. Publ. Mus. Zool. Univ. Mich.* 37:1–119.

Vehrencamp, S. L. 1982. Body temperatures of incubating versus non-incubating roadrunners. *Condor* 84:203–207.

Vehrencamp, S. L., and L. Halpenny. 1981. Capture and radio-transmitter attachment techniques for roadrunners. *North Am. Bird Bander* 6:128–32.

Visher, S. S. 1910. Notes on the birds of Pima Co., Arizona. *Auk* 27:279–88.

Webster, C. M. 2000. Distribution, habitat, and nests of the greater roadrunners in urban and suburban environments. Master's thesis, School of Renewable Natural Resources, Univ. Ariz., Tucson.

Wetmore, A. 1959. *Birds of the Pleistocene in North America*. Washington, D.C.: Smithson. Inst. Press.

———. 1968. *The birds of the Republic of Panama*. Pt. 2. Washington, D.C.: Smithson. Inst. Press.

Wheelock, G. 1904. *Birds of California*. 4th ed. A. C. McClurg and Co.

White, L. A. 1986. Notes on the ethnozoology of the Keresan Pueblo Indians. In *An ethnobiology sourcebook*, ed. R. I. Ford, pp. 223–27. New York: Garland.

Whitson, M. A. 1971. Field and laboratory investigations of the ethology of courtship and copulation in the greater roadrunner (*Geococcyx californianus*—Aves, Cuculidae). PhD diss., Univ. Okla., Norman.

———. 1975. Courtship behavior of the greater roadrunner. *Living Bird* 14:215–55.

———. 1983. The roadrunner: clown of the desert. *Natl. Geogr. Mag.* 163:694–702.

Wilks, B. J., and H. E. Laughlin. 1961. Roadrunner preys on a bat. *J. Mammal.* 42:98.

Willis, E. O. 1982. Ground cuckoos Aves Cuculidae as army ant followers. *Rev. Bras. Biol.* 42:753–56.

Willis, E. O., and Y. Oniki. 1978. Birds and army ants. *Annu. Rev. Ecol. Syst.* 9:243–63.

Wood, D. S., and G. D. Schnell. 1984. *Distributions of Oklahoma birds*. Norman: Univ. Okla. Press.

Woodard, D. W. 1975. Breeding bird communities in terrestrial habitats in the Coastal Bend region of Texas. Ph.D. dissertation, Univ. of Ark. Fayetteville.

Woodbury, A. M., and C. Cottam. 1962. Ecological studies of birds in Utah. *Univ. Utah Biol. Ser.* 12(7).

Woods, R. S. 1927. Road-runner versus mockingbird. *Condor* 22:273.

———. 1960. Notes on the nesting of the roadrunner. *Condor* 62:483–84.

Wright, B. 1973. *Kachinas, a Hopi artist's documentary*. Flagstaff, Ariz.: Northland Press.

———. 1977. *Hopi kachinas: the complete guide to collecting kachina dolls*. Flagstaff, Ariz.: Northland Press.

Wright, R. E. 1973. Observations on the urban feeding habits of the roadrunner (*Geococcyx californianus*). *Condor* 75:246.

Yarrow, H. C., H. W. Henshaw, and E. D. Cope. 1875. Reports upon the zoological collections obtained from portions of Nevada, Utah, California, Colorado, New Mexico, and Arizona. In *Report upon geographical and geological explorations and surveys west of the one hundredth meridian*. Eng. Dept., U.S. Army. Washington, D.C.: Gov. Printing Office.

Zimmerman, D. A. 1970. Roadrunner predation on passerine birds. *Condor* 72:475–76.

Index